chocolate

NEW HOLLAND

contents

introduction

From Aztec times people have enjoyed the taste provided by the seeds of the tropical cacao tree, called cocoa beans, which are the source of chocolate. Chocolate and cocoa are made from cocoa beans, the seeds of the tropical cacao tree. This tree originates from Central America, and is known scientifically as Theobroma cacao. Theobroma, meaning literally 'food of the gods', is a highly appropriate name for the cocoa bean, the source of such delicious cakes, biscuits, drinks and other sweets.

Since its discovery, the cocoa bean has to rate as one of the most influential foods of all time. Bahia, in eastern Brazil, and Ivory Coast currently produce almost half of the world's cocoa beans.

The beans in their original state are large oval fruits of many shapes and colours. When opened you will find a mass of tan-coloured seeds surrounded by a sticky whitish coloured pulp that has a sweet tartish flavour, reminiscent of lychees – certainly nothing like the end product of chocolate.

The processing of chocolate begins with the harvest of the pods of the cacao tree. During the production process, cocoa pods are harvested and then broken open, releasing the seeds. The beans are harvested and split, the white pulp is then squeezed out and allowed to ferment for 2–9 days to develop flavour. They are then spread onto wooden trays to dry in the sun. It takes about 4–5 days of drying time before the seeds are ready to be graded and bagged for sale.

The chocolate manufacturer generally blends seeds from several sources to produce a consistent style and desirable flavour. After cleaning and blending seeds, the manufacturer roasts them (something like roasting coffee) to develop flavour and aroma, before the seeds are shelled. The meat or 'nibs' are saved, the shells are sold for animal feed or fertiliser. The nibs, which are slightly more than 50% cocoa butter, are then ground to produce chocolate liquor. This is then used alone or blended with other ingredients to make specific types of chocolate or chocolate products.

In times past, the nibs were ground into a sticky paste and mixed with sugar and flour then rolled into balls about the size of a lime and allowed to dry. To make a tasty drink from these small balls, one grated the outside of the hard surface of the ball, dissolved the gratings in water or milk, then heated to make a thick chocolate drink.

Advances in processing over the years have resulted in the availability of a huge variety of wonderful products, from exquisite Swiss chocolates to warming cocoa drinks and quick pick-me-up chocolate bars.

Types of chocolate

Chocolate can be divided into four broad usage types: cooking chocolate, eating chocolate, cocoa powders and other chocolate products.

The quality of chocolate is based on the percentage of cocoa butter, which should always be listed on the label of the product, so check this before purchasing. The higher the percentage of cocoa butter content, the better the chocolate and higher the quality of your finished product.

Eating chocolate comes in a wide variety of flavours and fillings. It is generally sweeter than cooking chocolate, and is not as suitable for cooking. The amount of sugar added depends on the formula of the individual manufacturer. It is broadly divided into the following types: bittersweet, dark, milk and white.

Bittersweet chocolate
Bittersweet chocolate has a high percentage of cocoa liquor – 70% or above.

Dark chocolate
This is chocolate with a relatively high proportion of cocoa liquor, but less than 70%. In Britain this is known as plain chocolate, and in America as semi-sweet chocolate.

Milk chocolate
This is dark chocolate with more sugar and dried milk solids added. Widely used for chocolate bars and confectionery.

White chocolate

This is white-coloured 'chocolate' that lacks chocolate liquor, so technically is not real chocolate at all. It contains cocoa butter with added sugar, milk and flavourings, and should not be substituted for chocolate in recipes.

Cooking chocolate

Cooking chocolate generally has a higher proportion of cocoa butter and a lower proportion of sugar than eating chocolate. It is available in both dark and milk varieties as well as the varieties listed below.

Commercial coating or couverture chocolate

The highest grade of cooking chocolate, used by professional confectioners to make high-quality sweets and cake decorations, including curls, ruffles and other garnishes. It has more cocao butter than regular cooking chocolate, which allows it to melt and spread well, but makes it trickier for a non-professional to handle.

Solid unsweetened chocolate

This chocolate is bitter and unsuitable for eating. Professional chefs often use it in cooking as it gives them better control of the sugar content and flavour of the product.

Chocolate chips, buttons, buds or morsels

This is chocolate sold as small disks that contain a lower percentage of cocoa butter (about 29%) than chocolate bars. This helps them retain their shape when baked in biscuits and muffins. Available in dark, milk and white chocolate varieties.

Chocolate melts

Chocolate sold as small disks especially designed for non-professionals, as they are easy to work with when melted.

Compound chocolate

Compound chocolate, also called chocolate coating or compound coating chocolate, is an imitation product designed to replace high-quality chocolate in cooking. It can be purchased in block or disk form and in milk and dark varieties. Compound chocolate is made from a vegetable oil base combined with sugar, milk solids and flavouring. It contains cocoa powder but little or no cocoa butter and is easy to melt. It does not require tempering (see page 17) and so is the easiest form for beginners to work with.

Cocoa powders and drinking cocoa

Powdered cocoa is produced by pressing enough cocoa butter out of the chocolate liquor to leave a press cake with a content of 10–25% cocoa butter. It is used to make a variety of subsidiary products.

Dutch cocoa powder

This cocoa powder is produced by a method using an alkaline. The result is a smooth, rich and milder flavour than natural cocoa powder.

Unsweetened cocoa powder

This cocoa powder is less alkaline than Dutch cocoa, so care must be taken if substituting for Dutch cocoa in recipes. You may need to adjust levels of baking powder and baking soda to suit.

Basic technique

Drinking chocolate (powder)

This powder has milk solids and sugar added to cocoa powder to make it more palatable for drinking. It will not dissolve easily in cold liquids.

Instant cocoa products

These products usually contain lecithin or other emulsifiers that make cocoa easier to dissolve in cold liquids.

Chocolate-flavoured syrup

Sugar or corn syrup and cocoa blended with preservatives, emulsifiers and flavourings. Usually packed in bottles or cans and used for a topping for ice cream and desserts.

Storing chocolate

Chocolate should be stored in a dry, airy place at a temperature of about 16°C. If stored in unsuitable conditions, the cocoa butter in chocolate may rise to the surface, leaving a white film or 'bloom'. A similar discolouration occurs when water condenses on the surface. This can happen to refrigerated chocolates that have been too loosely wrapped. Chocolate affected in this way is still suitable for melting, but not for grating.

Melting chocolate

Chocolate melts more rapidly if broken into small pieces. The melting process should occur slowly since chocolate scorches if overheated. To melt chocolate, place the chocolate in the top of a double saucepan or in a bowl set over a saucepan of simmering water and heat, stirring, until chocolate melts and becomes smooth.

Alternatively, chocolate can be melted in the microwave. To melt 13oz (375g) chocolate, break it into small pieces and place in a microwavable glass or ceramic bowl or jug and cook on 100% for 1 minute. Stir. If the chocolate is not completely melted, cook for 30–45 seconds longer. When melting chocolate in the microwave, you should be aware that it holds its shape and it is important to stir it frequently so that it does not burn.

The container in which the chocolate is being melted should be kept uncovered and completely dry. Covering could cause condensation and just one drop of water will ruin the chocolate.

Chocolate 'seizes' if it is overheated, or if it comes into contact with water or steam. Seizing results in the chocolate tightening and becoming a thick mass that will not melt. To rescue seized chocolate, stir in a little cream or vegetable oil until the chocolate becomes smooth again.

Tempering chocolate

Tempering is a technique for stabilising chocolate that has been melted. It is a carefully controlled melting-and-cooling process, which allows the cocoa butter molecules to solidify in an orderly fashion and for the chocolate to harden properly.

When you melt chocolate, the molecules of fat separate (as cream separates from milk). Solidified, untempered chocolate will quickly acquire 'bloom', will not snap cleanly and is dull in appearance. Tempering returns the cocoa butter crystals to suspension within the chocolate and gives the chocolate a dark glossy appearance and a firm consistency.

Coarsely chop chocolate to be tempered. Also finely grate a few grams of unmelted semi-sweet or bittersweet coating chocolate. You will need 1 tablespoon grated chocolate for every 4oz (125g) of coarsely chopped chocolate. Melt chopped chocolate in a dry bowl set over hot water, stir until smooth. Do not allow chocolate to exceed 46°C – test with a thermometer. Remove bowl from hot water and set firmly on bench (on a towel is best). Gradually stir in grated chocolate, a spoonful at a time, stirring until melted before adding another spoonful. If the dipping chocolate is semi-sweet or bittersweet, cool to 86–90°F (30–32°C); if milk chocolate, cool to 82–88°F (28–31°C). Keep temperature constant by returning it to the warm water – if temperature drops too much mixture will be too thick to coat properly. Similarly, if temperature rises too high above 90°F (32°C), it will have to be re-tempered.

Making decorations

Chocolate leaves

To make chocolate leaves, choose non-poisonous, fresh, stiff leaves with raised veins. When picking, retain as much stem as possible. Wash leaves, then dry well on absorbent paper. Brush the underside of the leaves with melted chocolate and allow to set at room temperature. When set, carefully peel away leaf. Use one leaf to decorate an individual dessert, or a make a number and use to decorate a large dessert or cake.

Chocolate cases

To make chocolate cases for filled chocolates, quarter-fill a mould with melted chocolate and tap mould to remove any air bubbles. Brush chocolate evenly up sides of mould to make a shell, then freeze for 2 minutes or until set. Larger chocolate cases to hold desserts can also be made in this way using foil-lined individual metal flan tins, brioche tins or muffin tins as moulds. When set, remove from tins and fill with dessert filling such as mousse or a flavoured cream.

Chocolate caraque

Chocolate caraque is a layer of chocolate scrolls or flakes, used for example to decorate a Black Forest cake. This is made by spreading a layer of melted chocolate over a marble, granite or ceramic work surface. Allow the chocolate to set at room temperature. Then, holding a metal pastry scraper or a large knife at a 45° angle, slowly push it along the work surface away from you to form the chocolate into cylinders. If chocolate shavings form, then the chocolate is too cold and is best to start again.

Chocolate curls or shavings

Using a vegetable peeler, shave the sides of the chocolate. Whether curls or shavings form depends on the temperature of the chocolate. Chocolate curls are made from chocolate that is at room temperature. To make shavings, you need to use chilled chocolate.

Piped chocolate decorations

You can use piped chocolate decorations to decorate cakes, pastries and desserts – they are quick and easy to make.

Trace a simple design onto a sheet of paper. Tape a sheet of baking paper to your work surface and slide the drawings under the paper. Place melted chocolate into a paper or material piping bag (see page 17) and, following the tracings, pipe thin lines. Allow to set at room temperature and then carefully remove, using a metal spatula. If you are not going to use these decorations immediately, store them in an airtight container in a cool place.

Making a paper piping bag

Filling a piping bag

Spoon chocolate or frosting into the bag to half-full. Fold about 1cm of the bag over then fold over again. Fold the tips towards the centre and press your thumb on the join to force the chocolate or frosting out.

Using a piping bag

Grip the piping bag near the top with the folded or twisted end held between the thumb and fingers. Guide the bag with your free hand. Right-handed people should decorate from left to right, while left-handers need to decorate from right to left, except when piping writing.

The appearance of your piping will be directly affected by how you squeeze and relax your grip, that is, the pressure you apply and the steadiness of that pressure. The pressure should be so consistent that you can move the bag in a free and easy glide with just the right amount of chocolate or frosting flowing from the nozzle. A little practice will soon have you feeling confident.

Preparing a plastic bag for piping

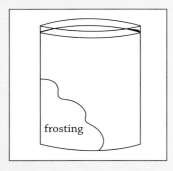

1. Take a sturdy, small- to medium-size plastic bag, place the frosting or warm chocolate into one corner and gently remove any air from the bag.

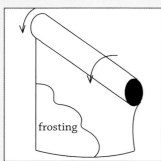

2. Fold over then roll down the top of the plastic bag on a diagonal angle, toward the filled corner that you will write from.

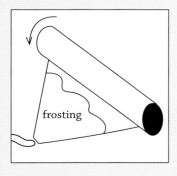

3. Snip a small piece of plastic from the corner of the bag to allow the frosting to flow. Control the frosting by applying more or less pressure to the rolled-up back part of the bag.

Making a paper piping bag

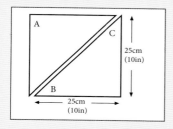

1. Cut a 10in (25cm) square of baking paper. Cut the square in half diagonally to form two triangles. To make the piping bag, place the paper triangles on top of each other and mark the three corners A, B and C.

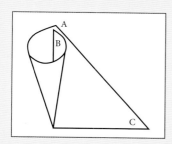

2. Fold corner B around and inside corner A.

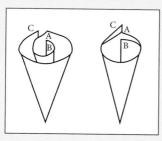

3. Bring corner C around the outside of the bag until it fits exactly behind corner A. At this stage all three corners should be together and the point closed.

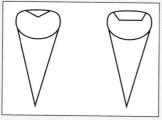

4. Fold corner A over two or three times to hold the bag together. Snip the point off the bag and drop into an frosting nozzle. The piping bag can also be used without a nozzle for writing and outlines, in which case only the very tip of the point should be snipped off.

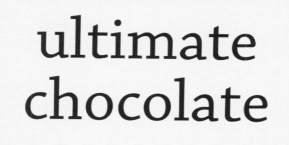

ultimate
chocolate

Rich devil's food cake

serves 8

1. Place butter and superfine sugar in a bowl and beat until light and fluffy. Gradually beat in eggs.

2. Sift together flour, cocoa powder and baking powder over butter mixture. Add milk and a few drops of food colouring and mix well to combine. Pour mixture into two buttered and lined 7¾in (20cm) round cake tins and bake for 45 minutes or until cooked when tested with a skewer. Stand cakes in tins for 5 minutes before turning onto wire racks to cool.

3. To make filling, place cream in a bowl and beat until soft peaks form. Fold in chocolate.

4. To assemble cake, place one cake on a serving plate. Spread with jam and filling and top with remaining cake. Just prior to serving, dust top of cake with powdered sugar. Cut a template of a devil's fork from baking paper. Lay template on top of cake and dust with cocoa powder.

6oz (185g) butter, softened
1¾ cups superfine (caster) sugar
3 eggs
2 cups all-purpose (plain) flour
⅔ cup cocoa powder
1½ teaspoons baking powder
1 cup milk
few drops red food colouring
½ cup raspberry jam
2 tablespoons cocoa powder,
    for dusting
CHOCOLATE CREAM
    FILLING
½ cup double cream
3oz (90g) dark chocolate, melted
and cooled

Ultimate chocolate sundae

serves 6

1. Preheat oven to 350°F (180°C). To make base, place butter, eggs, superfine sugar and vanilla in a bowl and beat to combine. Add flour, cocoa powder, and pecans and mix well to combine.

2. Pour mixture into a buttered and lined 7¾in (20cm) square cake tin and bake for 30 minutes or until firm to touch, but still fudgy in the centre. Cool in tin, then cut into six squares.

3. To make sauce, place brown sugar, cocoa powder, cream and butter in a saucepan and cook over a low heat, stirring constantly, until sugar dissolves. Bring to the boil, then reduce heat and simmer for 5 minutes or until sauce thickens slightly.

4. To assemble sundaes, top each brownie square with a scoop of vanilla, chocolate and choc chip ice cream. Drizzle with hot sauce and serve.

6 scoops vanilla ice cream
6 scoops chocolate ice cream
6 scoops choc-chip ice cream
BROWNIE BASE
9oz (250g) butter, melted
4 eggs, lightly beaten
1¼ cups superfine (caster) sugar
2 teaspoons vanilla extract
¾ cup all-purpose (plain) flour, sifted
¼ cup cocoa powder, sifted
1½oz (45g) pecans, chopped
FUDGE SAUCE
2 cups brown sugar
¼ cup cocoa powder, sifted
1 cup double cream
1oz (30g) butter

Chocolate profiteroles

serves 6–8

7oz (200g) dark chocolate, melted

CHOUX PASTRY

3oz (90g) butter

1 cup all-purpose (plain) flour

3 eggs

CHOCOLATE LIQUEUR FILLING

½ cup sugar

3 egg yolks

2 tablespoons all-purpose (plain) flour

1 cup milk

2oz (60g) dark chocolate, broken into pieces

1 tablespoon orange-flavoured liqueur

1. Preheat oven to 400°F (200°C). To make pastry, place, 1 cup water the butter in a saucepan and slowly bring to the boil. As soon as the mixture boils, quickly stir in flour. Cook over a low heat, stirring constantly, for 2 minutes or until mixture is smooth and leaves sides of pan.

2. Beat in eggs one at a time, beating well after each addition, until mixture is light and glossy.

3. Place heaped tablespoonfuls of mixture on baking trays and bake for 10 minutes. Reduce oven temperature to 350°F (180°C) and cook for 10 minutes longer or until golden and crisp. Pierce a small hole in the base of each pastry and transfer to wire racks to cool.

4. To make filling, place sugar and egg yolks in a bowl and beat until thick and pale. Add flour and beat until combined.

5. Place milk, chocolate and liqueur in a a saucepan and heat over a medium heat, stirring constantly, until mixture is smooth. Remove from heat and slowly stir in egg yolk mixture. Return to heat and cook over medium heat, stirring constantly, until mixture thickens. Remove pan from heat, cover and set aside.

6. Place filling in a piping bag fitted with a plain small nozzle and pipe filling through hole in base of profiteroles. Dip tops in melted dark chocolate and place on a wire rack to set.

Sacher torte

serves 8–10

9oz (250g) butter, softened
1½cups brown sugar
2 teaspoons vanilla extract
2 eggs, lightly beaten
1½ cups all-purpose (plain) flour
⅔ cup cocoa powder
¾ teaspoon baking powder
1½ cups buttermilk
½ cup apricot jam
DARK CHOCOLATE
  FROSTING
7oz (200g) dark chocolate,
  broken into pieces
7oz (200g) butter, chopped

1. Preheat oven to 350°F (180°C). Place butter, sugar and vanilla in a bowl and beat until light and fluffy. Gradually beat in eggs.

2. Sift flour, cocoa powder and baking powder into butter mixture. Add buttermilk and mix well to combine.

3. Pour mixture into two buttered and lined 9in (23cm) cake tins and bake for 25 minutes or until cooked when tested with a skewer. Stand in tins for 5 minutes before turning onto wire racks to cool.

4. To make frosting, place chocolate and butter in a heatproof bowl set over a saucepan of simmering water and heat, stirring, until mixture is smooth. Remove bowl from pan and set aside to cool until mixture thickens and is of a spreadable consistency.

5. To assemble cake, place one cake on a serving plate and spread with jam. Top with remaining cake and spread top and sides with frosting. Place remaining frosting in a piping bag and pipe swirls around edge of cake.

Chocolate ice cream

serves 8

1. Place sugar and egg yolks in a bowl and beat until thick and pale.

2. Place cocoa powder in a saucepan. Gradually stir in milk and cream and heat over a medium heat, stirring constantly, until mixture is almost boiling. Stir in chocolate.

3. Remove pan from heat and whisk hot milk mixture into egg mixture. Set aside to cool.

4. Pour mixture into a freezerproof container and freeze for 30 minutes or until mixture begins to freeze around edges. Beat mixture until even in texture. Return to freezer and repeat beating process two more times. Freeze until solid.

NOTE

For true chocoholics, chopped chocolate or chocolate bits can be folded into the mixture before it freezes solid. Serve in scoops with vanilla tuiles or raspberries.

1 cup superfine (caster) sugar
9 egg yolks
½ cup cocoa powder, sifted
2 cups milk
2½ cups double cream
½ cup milk chocolate, melted

Chocolate soufflé

serves 6

1. Preheat oven to 375°F (190°C). Place chocolate and half the cream in a heatproof bowl set over a saucepan of simmering water and heat, stirring constantly, until mixture is smooth. Remove bowl from pan and set aside to cool slightly.

2. Place egg yolks and superfine sugar in a clean bowl and beat until thick and pale. Gradually beat in flour and remaining cream and beat until combined.

3. Transfer egg yolk mixture to a saucepan and cook over a medium heat, stirring constantly, for 5 minutes or until mixture thickens. Remove pan from heat and stir in chocolate mixture.

4. Place egg whites in a clean bowl and beat until stiff peaks form. Fold egg whites into chocolate mixture. Divide mixture evenly between six buttered and sugared one-cup capacity soufflé dishes and bake for 25 minutes or until soufflés are puffed. Dust with powdered sugar and serve immediately.

NOTE

To prepare soufflé dishes, brush interior of each with melted unsalted butter, coating lightly and evenly, then sprinkle lightly with superfine sugar.

9oz (250g) dark chocolate, broken into pieces
1 cup double cream
6 eggs, separated
1 cup superfine (caster) sugar
¼ cup all-purpose (plain) flour
¼ cup powdered (icing) sugar, sifted

Black forest gâteau

serves 6–8

7oz (200g) dark chocolate,
  chopped
3 cups self-rising (self-raising)
  flour
1 cup superfine (caster) sugar
¼ cup cocoa powder
1½ cups milk
3 eggs, lightly beaten
6oz (185g) butter, softened
2 tablespoons cherry brandy
chocolate curls, to decorate (see
  page 14)
CHERRY CREAM FILLING
2 cups double cream
⅓ cup superfine (caster) sugar
15oz (440g) canned pitted
  cherries, well drained

1.   Preheat oven to 350°F (180°C). Place chocolate in a heatproof bowl set over a saucepan of simmering water and heat, stirring, until chocolate melts. Remove bowl from pan and set aside to cool slightly.

2.   Sift together flour, sugar and cocoa powder into a bowl. Add milk, eggs and butter and beat for 5 minutes or until mixture is smooth. Beat in chocolate until mixture is well combined.

3.   Pour mixture into a deep, buttered 9in (23cm) round cake tin and bake for 60 minutes or until cooked when tested with a skewer. Stand in tin for 5 minutes before turning onto a wire rack to cool.

4.   To make filling, place cream and sugar in a bowl and beat until soft peaks form. Divide cream into two portions. Fold cherries into one portion.

5.   To assemble cake, using a serrated edged knife, cut cake into three even layers. Sprinkle each layer with cherry brandy. Place one layer of cake on a serving plate, spread with half the cherry cream and top with a second layer of cake. Spread with remaining cherry cream and top with remaining layer of cake. Spread top and sides of cake with cream. Decorate top of cake with chocolate curls.

Chocolate torte

serves 10–12

5½oz (160g) dark chocolate,
  broken into pieces
1 cup brown sugar
½ cup double cream
2 egg yolks
7oz (200g) butter, softened
1 cup sugar
1 teaspoon vanilla extract
2 eggs, lightly beaten
1 cup all-purpose (plain) flour
1 cup self-rising (self-raising)
  flour
¾ cup milk
3 egg whites
3oz (90g) flaked almonds,
  toasted
chocolate-drizzled strawberries
RICH CHOCOLATE
  FROSTING
¾ cup sugar
6 egg yolks
7oz (200g) dark chocolate,
  melted
9oz (250g) butter, chopped

1. Preheat oven to 350°F (180°C). Place first 4 ingredients in a heatproof bowl set over a saucepan of simmering water. Stir until mixture is smooth. Set aside to cool slightly.

2. Place butter, sugar and vanilla in a bowl and beat until light and fluffy. Gradually beat in the eggs. Sift together flour and self-rising flour over butter mixture. Add chocolate mixture and milk and mix until well combined.

3. Place egg whites in a clean bowl and beat until stiff peaks form. Fold egg whites into chocolate mixture. Pour mixture into two buttered and lined 9in (23cm) round cake tins and bake for 40 minutes or until cooked. Stand in tins for 5 minutes before turning onto wire racks.

4. To make frosting, place sugar and ¾ cup water in a saucepan and heat, stirring constantly, until sugar dissolves. Bring to the boil, then reduce heat and simmer until mixture is syrupy.

5. Place egg yolks in a bowl and beat until thick and pale. Gradually beat in sugar syrup and melted chocolate. Then beat in butter and beat until mixture is thick. Cover and refrigerate.

6. To assemble, split each cake horizontally. Place one layer of cake on a serving plate and spread with frosting. Top with a second layer of cake and frosting. Repeat layers using remaining cake. Spread top and sides of cake with remaining frosting. Decorate with almonds and top with chocolate-drizzled strawberries.

Self-saucing pudding

serves 6

1. Preheat oven to 350°F (180°C). Sift together flour and cocoa powder in a bowl. Add superfine sugar and mix to combine. Make a well in the centre of the dry ingredients, add milk and butter and mix well to combine. Pour mixture into a buttered 4-cup capacity ovenproof dish.

2. To make sauce, place brown sugar and cocoa powder in a bowl. Gradually add 1¼ cups hot water and mix until smooth. Carefully pour sauce over mixture in dish and bake for 40 minutes or until cooked when tested with a skewer.

3. Serve scoops of pudding with some of the sauce from the base of the dish and top with a scoop of vanilla or chocolate ice cream.

1 cup self-rising (self-raising) flour
¼ cup cocoa powder
¾ cup superfine (caster) sugar
½ cup milk
1½oz (45g) butter, melted
CHOCOLATE SAUCE
¾ cup brown sugar
¼ cup cocoa powder, sifted

Chocolate mousse with fresh berries

serves 6

1. Put the chocolate in an ovenproof bowl over a pot of simmering water, making sure the base of the bowl does not come in contact with the water and that no water touches the chocolate. Stir over a low heat until the chocolate melts then set aside to cool slightly.

2. Put the gelatine and 4 tablespoons water into a small pot and stir over a low heat until the gelatine dissolves and the liquid is clear. Remove from the heat and allow to cool slightly.

3. Beat the ricotta and custard together until smooth. Press through a sieve to remove any lumps. Beat egg whites until light and fluffy, then set aside.

4. Fold the gelatine and chocolate into the ricotta, then fold in the beaten egg whites. Spoon the mousse into 6 half-cup ramekins or mugs, cover and refrigerate for 1 hour or until set. Serve with the berries.

6oz (170g) bittersweet chocolate, chopped
2 teaspoons powdered gelatine
3½oz (100g) ricotta cheese
1 cup reduced-fat vanilla custard
4 egg whites
10½oz (300g) mixed fresh berries

Dark chocolate mousse

serves 8–12

14oz (400g) dark chocolate
4 tablespoons orange juice
zest of 2 oranges
8 eggs, separated
4 tablespoons superfine (caster)
  sugar
1¾oz (50g) butter

1. Chop or grate the chocolate and then melt slowly with the orange juice in a bowl over simmering water.

2. Remove from heat and beat in the egg yolks and orange zest. Continue beating until the mixture is thick and well combined.

3. Beat the egg whites until frothy, then add the sugar while continuing to beat until thick and glossy. Fold the egg whites into the chocolate mixture. Pipe or pour into dishes and chill for 4 hours or overnight. Decorate with caramelised orange zest if desired.

cakes

Individual dessert cakes

serves 6

1. Preheat oven to 350°F (180°C). Place chocolate and butter in a heatproof bowl set over a saucepan of simmering water and heat, stirring, until mixture is smooth. Remove bowl from pan and set aside to cool.

2. Place eggs, egg yolks, and sugar in a bowl and beat until thick and pale. Gradually beat in flour and chocolate mixture and beat well. Divide mixture evenly between six buttered small fluted brioche moulds or small ramekins, place on a baking tray and bake for 12–15 minutes or until cakes are just firm – the centres should still be soft and fudgy. Turn onto serving plates and dust with cocoa powder.

NOTE

Delicious served with spiced mascarpone or ice cream and chocolate sauce. To make spiced mascarpone, fold 1 tablespoon finely chopped crystallised ginger, 1 tablespoon honey and ground mixed spice to taste into 13oz (375g) mascarpone. Chill until ready to serve.

3½oz (100g) dark chocolate, broken into pieces
4oz (125g) butter, chopped
2 eggs plus 2 egg yolks
⅓ cup sugar
2 tablespoons all-purpose (plain) flour
cocoa powder, for dusting

Austrian maple spice cake

serves 12

1. Preheat oven to 340°F (170°C). Butter a non-stick 11in (28cm) or 10¹/₃in (26cm) springform tin and set aside.

2. In a large bowl, mix together the flour, baking powder, cinnamon, cloves, ginger and cocoa. In a separate bowl, whisk the maple syrup, honey, sugar, buttermilk and vanilla. Gently but thoroughly combine the flour mixture and the syrup mixture.

3. Pour the batter into the prepared cake tin and bake for 1 hour and 10 minutes, until springy when pressed gently in the centre. When cooked, remove from the oven and cool thoroughly. Remove from tin and set aside.

4. To make the glaze, melt the chocolate and butter, in a bowl resting over a saucepan of simmering water. When melted, whisk in the orange juice thoroughly. Meanwhile, warm the marmalade and gently spread it over the surface of the cake. Allow to cool.

5. When the chocolate mixture is smooth, carefully pour it over the marmalade-topped cake and spread it to cover.

6. Cut the zest of the orange into long fine strips. Heat the sugar and 2 teaspoons water together in a small saucepan, add the zest and simmer for 5 minutes. Lift out the caramelised zest and allow to cool. Discard the syrup. Pile the orange zest and chocolate shavings in the centre of the cake.

3 cups all-purpose (plain) flour
3 teaspoons baking powder
2 tablespoons ground cinnamon
1 teaspoon ground cloves
2 teaspoons ground ginger
2 tablespoons Dutch cocoa powder
1 cup pure maple syrup
½ cup honey
1½ cups superfine (caster) sugar
1½ cups buttermilk
1 teaspoon vanilla extract
2 tablespoons chocolate shavings, for garnish

GLAZE
7oz (200g) dark cooking chocolate
1oz (30g) butter
juice and zest of 1 small orange
3 tablespoons marmalade
4 tablespoons sugar

Simple chocolate cake

serves 8

4oz (125g) butter, softened
1 cup sugar
1 teaspoon vanilla extract
2 eggs, lightly beaten
1¼ cups self-rising (self-raising)
  flour
½ cup cocoa powder
1 teaspoon baking soda
1 cup milk
gold or silver dragees
CHOCOLATE BUTTER
  FROSTING
4oz (125g) dark chocolate
2oz (60g) butter
¼ cup double cream

1. Preheat oven to 350°F (180°C). Place butter, sugar and vanilla in a bowl and beat until light and fluffy. Gradually beat in eggs.
2. Sift flour, cocoa powder and baking soda together into a bowl. Fold flour mixture and milk alternately into egg mixture.
3. Pour mixture into a buttered and lined 18cm square cake tin and bake for 40 minutes or until cooked when tested with a skewer. Stand in tin for 5 minutes before turning onto a wire rack to cool.
4. To make frosting, place chocolate, butter and cream in a heatproof bowl set over a saucepan of simmering water and heat, stirring constantly, until mixture is smooth. Remove bowl from pan and set aside to cool slightly. Spread top and sides of cake with frosting and decorate with gold or silver dragees.

NOTE

This basic butter cake is a good one for baking in muffin or patty tins for individual servings in school or office lunch boxes. Fill tins two-thirds full with batter and bake until cooked when tested with a skewer. Drizzle with a simple glacé frosting when cold.

Mississippi mud cake

serves 12

9oz (250g) butter, chopped
   coarsely
7oz (200g) dark eating chocolate,
   chopped coarsely
1⅓ cups milk
2 cups superfine (caster) sugar
1 teaspoon vanilla extract
1½ cups all-purpose (plain) flour
¼ cup self-rising (self-raising)
   flour
¼ cup cocoa
2 eggs
DARK CHOCOLATE
   GANACHE
⅓ cup cream
7oz (200g) dark eating chocolate,
   chopped coarsely

1.   Preheat oven to 340°F (170°C). Grease deep 8½in (22cm) round cake pan; line base with baking paper.

2.   Combine butter, chocolate, milk, sugar and extract in medium saucepan, stir over low heat until mixture is smooth.

3.   Cool mixture until barely warm, whisk in sifted dry ingredients and eggs. Pour mixture into pan, bake about 1½ hours. Stand cake for 5 minutes before turning onto wire rack to cool.

4.   To make dark chocolate ganache, bring cream to the boil in small saucepan, remove from heat and add chocolate, stir until smooth, then pour over the cake. You could also refrigerate the ganache for about 30 minutes, beat with a wooden spoon or mixer until smooth and then spread over cake.

Frangelico chocolate cake with raspberry sauce

serves 8

1. Preheat the oven to 375°F (190°C). Melt the chocolate and butter over hot water, remove from the heat, and stir in the egg yolks, sugar, flour, baking powder, hazelnuts and Frangelico.

2. Beat the egg whites until soft peaks form. Fold egg whites lightly into the chocolate mixture and pour into a buttered and lined round 7¾in (20cm) cake tin. Bake for 40–45 minutes or until the cake shrinks slightly from the sides of the tin.

3. To make the sauce, place the raspberries, powdered sugar and lemon juice in a food processor and blend until smooth. Strain and add a little water if the mixture is too thick.

4. Serve the cake cut into wedges, with raspberry sauce and cream. Dust with powdered sugar.

7oz (200g) bittersweet chocolate, chopped
3½oz (100g) butter
5 eggs, separated
½ cup superfine (caster) sugar
⅓ cup all-purpose (plain) flour, sifted
⅓ teaspoon baking powder
½ cup ground hazelnuts
¼ cup Frangelico liqueur
1 tablespoon powdered (icing) sugar, for dusting

SAUCE
4oz (125g) raspberries
2 tablespoons powdered (icing) sugar, sifted
1 tablespoon lemon juice

Chocolate pound cake

serves 8

1. Preheat oven to 375°F (190°C). Place butter, sugar and vanilla in a bowl and beat until light and fluffy. Gradually beat in eggs.

2. Sift together self-rising flour, flour and cocoa powder. Fold flour mixture and milk alternately into butter mixture.

3. Pour mixture into a buttered and lined 7¾in (20cm) square cake tin and bake for 55 minutes or until cooked when tested with a skewer. Stand in tin for 10 minutes before turning onto a wire rack to cool. Serve with chocolate sauce and cream. Dust with powdered sugar.

6oz (185g) butter, softened
1¼ cups superfine (caster) sugar
3 teaspoons vanilla extract
3 eggs, lightly beaten
1½ cups self-rising (self-raising) flour
½ cup all-purpose (plain) flour
½ cup cocoa powder
1¼ cups milk
powdered (icing) sugar, for dusting

Grandma's chocolate cake

serves 8

4oz (125g) butter, softened
2 cups superfine (caster) sugar
2 eggs
2 teaspoons vanilla extract
1 cup self-rising (self-raising)
    flour
¾ cup all-purpose (plain) flour
¾ cup cocoa powder
1 cup buttermilk
¾ cup raspberry jam
CHOCOLATE SOUR CREAM
    FILLING
6oz (185g) dark chocolate,
    broken into pieces
4oz (125g) butter, chopped
3¼ cups powdered (icing) sugar,
    sifted
½ cup sour cream

1. Preheat oven to 350°F (180°C). Place butter, superfine sugar, eggs and vanilla in a bowl and beat until light and fluffy. Sift together self-rising flour, flour and cocoa powder.

2. Fold flour mixture and buttermilk alternately into butter mixture. Divide mixture between four buttered and lined 9in (23cm) round cake tins and bake for 25 minutes or until cooked when tested with a skewer. Turn onto wire racks to cool.

3. To make filling, place chocolate and butter in a heatproof bowl set over a saucepan of simmering water and heat, stirring, until mixture is smooth. Remove bowl from pan. Add powdered sugar and sour cream and mix until smooth.

4. To assemble cake, place one cake on a serving plate and spread with some jam and top with some filling. Top with a second cake, some more jam and filling. Repeat layers until all cakes and jam are used. Finish with a layer of cake and spread remaining filling over top and sides of cake.

Chocolate espresso cheesecake

serves 12

CRUST

1 cup chocolate biscuit crumbs

2 tablespoons melted butter

1 tablespoon sugar

FILLING

9oz (250g) bittersweet chocolate, chopped

36oz (1kg) cream cheese

1 cup sugar

1 cup sour cream

2 large eggs

2 egg yolks

¼ cup espresso coffee

1 teaspoon vanilla extract

1 tablespoon freshly ground coffee

GANACHE

1 cup double cream

5½oz (160g) bittersweet chocolate, chopped

1 tablespoon instant espresso, dissolved in 2 tablespoons water

1. Make the crust by mixing together all of the crust ingredients in a bowl.

2. Press into the bottom of a 9in (23cm) springform tin. Ser aside and refrigerate until ready to use.

3. Make the filling by melting the chocolate in the top of a double boiler, then set aside to cool.

4. Cream the cream cheese and sugar until light and fluffy. Add the sour cream and mix, scraping down the sides of the bowl. Add eggs and egg yolks until well mixed. Then add the espresso, vanilla and ground coffee. Add chocolate and blend.

5. When well mixed pour mixture into prepared crust and place spring form in a water bath. Bake at 350°F (180°C) for 45 minutes.

6. When cooked turn off oven for about one hour before removing.

7. Make the ganache; bring cream to the boil on stove. Then pour over the chopped chocolate and let stand for about one minute. Stir to dissolve, then stir in the espresso.

8. Let cool at room temperature. Pour over top of cooled cheesecake, refrigerate to let set.

Chocolate hazelnut torte

serves 8

1. Preheat the oven to 375°F (190°C). Place chocolate in a heatproof bowl set over a saucepan of simmering water and heat, stirring, until chocolate melts. Remove bowl from pan and cool slightly.

2. Place egg yolks and sugar in a bowl and beat until thick and pale. Fold chocolate, hazelnuts and rum into egg mixture.

3. Place egg whites into a clean bowl and beat until stiff peaks form. Fold egg whites into chocolate mixture. Pour mixture into a buttered and lined 9in (23cm) springform tin and bake for 50 minutes or until cooked when tested with a skewer. Cool cake in tin. Just prior to serving, dust cake with powdered sugar.

NOTE

To toast hazelnuts, place nuts on a baking tray and bake for 10 minutes or until skins begin to split. Place on a tea towel and rub to remove skins. Place in a food processor and process to roughly chop.

9oz (250g) dark chocolate, broken into pieces
6 eggs, separated
1 cup sugar
11½oz (325g) hazelnuts, toasted and roughly chopped
1 tablespoon rum
powdered (icing) sugar, for dusting

Choc meringue cake

serves 10

1. Preheat oven to 250°F (120°C). To make meringue, mix together ground hazelnuts, cornflour and ¾ cup sugar. Beat egg whites until soft peaks form, add remaining sugar a little at a time and beat until thick and glossy. Fold into hazelnut mixture.

2. Mark three 7¾in (20cm) squares on baking paper and place paper on baking trays. Place meringue mixture in a piping bag fitted (see page 17) with a small plain nozzle and pipe mixture to outline squares, then fill squares with piped lines of mixture. Bake for 40–50 minute or until crisp and dry.

3. To make filling, beat butter until soft. Add chocolate, superfine sugar and cream and beat until thick. Fold in brandy and hazelnuts.

4. To make topping, place chocolate and oil in the top of a double saucepan and heat over simmering water, stirring until chocolate melts and mixture is smooth. Remove top pan and set aside to cool.

5. To assemble cake, place a layer of meringue on a serving plate and spread with half the filling. Top with another meringue layer and most of the remaining filling. Cut remaining meringue into squares and position at angles on top of cake. Drizzle with last of the topping and decorate with cream and strawberries.

HAZELNUT MERINGUE
5½oz (160g) ground hazelnuts
2 tablespoons cornflour
1¼ cups sugar
6 egg whites
CHOCOLATE FILLING
7¾oz (220g) unsalted butter
6oz (185g) dark chocolate, melted
3 tablespoons superfine (caster) sugar
2 cups thickened cream
2 tablespoons brandy
4oz (125g) ground hazelnuts
CHOCOLATE TOPPING
5½oz (160g) dark chocolate
2 teaspoons vegetable oil
½ cup whipped cream
8 strawberries, halved

Chocolate babka

serves 6

9oz (250g) all-purpose (plain)
flour
4 tablespoons cocoa powder
1½ teaspoons baking powder
¾ teaspoon baking soda
(bicarbonate soda)
½ teaspoon salt
9oz (250g) butter
9oz (250g) powdered (icing)
sugar, sifted
1 teaspoon vanilla extract
4 eggs, separated
1 cup sour cream
TOPPING
1 cup chocolate chips
3 tablespoons superfine (caster)
sugar
4 tablespoons raisins
½ cup chopped pecan nuts

1. Preheat oven to 350°F (180°C). Grease a 9¾in (25cm) tube cake pan.

2. Sift together first 5 ingredients, then set aside. In a medium bowl, beat butter and sugar together with a mixer until light and fluffy. Then beat in the vanilla extract.

3. Beat the eggs in one at a time. With mixer on slow speed, alternately beat the flour mixture and sour cream into the creamed mixture, beginning and ending with the flour mixture. Beat until just blended, do not over-beat.

4. Make the topping by taking a small bowl and combining all of the topping ingredients to make a crumb mixture.

5. Spread half of the cake mixture in the bottom of the prepared pan. Sprinkle with half of the crumb mixture.Pour in the remaining cake mixture and sprinkle with the remaining topping mixture. Press the crumb mixture in tightly so that it sticks to the cake.

6. Cut through the cake and crumbs in an up and down motion with a kitchen knife, then tap down to settle.

7. Bake in the preheated oven for 40 minutes, then cover the top of cake with aluminium foil and bake for a further 20 minutes.

8. Leave the cake in the tin for about 30 minutes to allow to cool, then turn onto a cooling rack.

Coconut cake with fudge sauce

serves 8

4oz (125g) butter, softened
1 cup sugar
1 teaspoon vanilla extract
4 eggs, lightly beaten
6oz (185g) desiccated coconut
1 cup self-rising (self-raising)
  flour, sifted
⅓ cup sour cream
chocolate curls, to decorate (see
  page 14)
FUDGE SAUCE
2oz (60g) milk chocolate, broken
  into pieces
1oz (30g) butter, chopped
2 tablespoons golden syrup
1 cup sugar
¾ cup double cream

1. Preheat oven to 320°F (160°C). Place butter, sugar and vanilla in a bowl and beat until light and fluffy. Gradually beat in eggs. Stir coconut, flour and sour cream into butter mixture and mix until combined.

2. Pour mixture into a buttered and lined 7¾in (20cm) round cake tin and bake for 35 minutes. Stand in tin while making sauce.

3. To make sauce, place chocolate, butter and golden syrup in a saucepan and heat over a low heat, stirring, until mixture is smooth. Add sugar and cream and cook, stirring, until sugar dissolves. Bring to the boil, then reduce heat and simmer for 8 minutes or until sauce thickens. Serve with warm cake.

NOTE
Leftover fudge sauce can be stored in a covered container in the refrigerator. Reheat sauce in a heatproof bowl set over hot water and stir until smooth.

Caramel orange cheesecake

serves 8–10

1. Preheat oven to 320°F (160°C). Remove zest from oranges and set aside. Remove white pith from oranges. Cut oranges crosswise into ¼in- (1cm) thick slices. Place rum and brown sugar in a bowl and mix to combine. Add orange slices and set aside to stand for 1 hour.

2. To make base, combine biscuit crumbs, butter and superfine sugar in a bowl. Press mixture over base and up sides of a buttered and lined 7¾in (20cm) springform tin.

3. To make filling, place cream cheese, ricotta cheese, sugar, cream, sour cream, eggs, flour, orange zest and orange flower water or orange juice into a food processor and process until smooth.

4. Pour filling into tin and bake for 50 minutes or until firm. Cool in tin.

5. Place sugar and ¼ cup water in a saucepan and heat over a low heat, stirring, until sugar dissolves. Bring to the boil, then reduce heat and simmer until syrup is golden. Drain orange slices and arrange attractively on top of cheesecake. Pour sauce over cheesecake and serve, immediately.

3 oranges
½ cup rum
½ cup brown sugar
½ cup white sugar
CHOCOLATE BASE
9oz (250g) plain chocolate
  biscuits, crushed
4oz (125g) butter, melted
2 tablespoons superfine (caster)
  sugar
ORANGE FILLING
9oz (250g) cream cheese
4oz (125g) ricotta cheese
½ cup sugar
1 cup double cream
⅔ cup sour cream
3 eggs, lightly beaten
2 tablespoons all-purpose (plain)
  flour
zest of 2 large oranges, finely
  grated
1 tablespoon orange flower water
  or orange juice

Chocolate cheesecake

serves 8

1. To make the base, place the biscuits into a plastic bag then crush with a rolling pin to make crumbs. Place in a large bowl, then mix in the butter and sugar. Add the cinnamon and mix again. Press the mixture evenly into the base and up the sides of a 9in (23cm) loose-bottomed flan tin. Refrigerate until needed.

2. Preheat the oven to 350°F (180°C). In a large bowl, beat the cream cheese with a wooden spoon until soft and fluffy. Lightly beat the eggs in a small bowl, then gradually beat them into the cheese with the superfine sugar. Stir until the mixture is smooth. Set aside.

3. Melt the chocolate in a small bowl set over a saucepan of simmering water, stirring frequently. Remove from the heat and stir in the sour cream and rum. Mix well.

4. Stir the chocolate mixture into the cheese mixture, then pour over the cookie base. Bake for 30 minutes or until the edges look set (the middle may still look moist). Turn the heat off and leave the cheesecake to cool for 1 hour in the oven, with the door open.

5. Place the cheesecake in the refrigerator for 2 hours. Arrange strawberries around the edge of the cheesecake before serving.

BASE
7oz (200g) digestive biscuits
3½oz (100g) unsalted butter, at
    room temperature
1 tablespoon white sugar
¼ teaspoon ground cinnamon
FILLING
14oz (400g) cream cheese, at
    room temperature
2 eggs
5oz (145g) superfine (caster)
    sugar
7oz (200g) bittersweet chocolate,
    broken into pieces
5fl oz (145ml) sour cream
1 tablespoon dark rum
4oz (115g) strawberries, halved

Rich dark chocolate cake

serves 20

17½oz (500g) milk chocolate, broken into pieces
14oz (400g) unsalted butter
12oz (350g) superfine (caster) sugar
6 tablespoons all-purpose (plain) flour
6 large eggs, separated
pinch of salt
4oz (125g) fresh raspberries, to serve
20 sprigs mint, to serve
4oz (125g) icing sugar, for dusting
COATING
6 tablespoons seedless raspberry or cherry jam
7oz (200g) milk chocolate, broken into pieces
4 tablespoons cream
2 tablespoons pure powdered (icing) sugar

1. Preheat the oven to 400°F (200°C). Butter two 32oz (900g) loaf tins. Melt the chocolate with the butter, sugar and 3 tablespoons water in a bowl set over a saucepan of simmering water. Sift in the flour and stir, then beat in the egg yolks.

2. Place the egg whites into a bowl with a pinch of salt. Whisk until the mixture forms stiff peaks – this is easiest with an electric whisk. Fold 1 tablespoon of the whites into the chocolate mixture to loosen it, then fold in the remaining whites.

3. Divide the mixture between the tins and tap on the work surface to settle the contents. Bake for 45 minutes or until firm. Cool for 15 minutes in the tins. Turn out onto a cooling rack and leave for 2 hours or until cooled completely.

4. For the coating, heat the jam with 3 tablespoons of water in a pan until dissolved. Brush over the tops and sides of the cakes. Melt the chocolate with 3 tablespoons of water in a bowl set over a pan of simmering water, then stir in the cream and sugar. Smooth over the top and sides of the cakes, then place in the refrigerator for 1 hour. Decorate with raspberries and mint and dust with icing sugar. Serve with cream.

Muddy mud cake

serves 6

8oz (225g) butter, softened
8oz (225g) bittersweet chocolate,
  chopped
3½oz (100g) superfine (caster)
  sugar
3oz (85g) brown sugar
1½ tablespoons brandy
7oz (200g) all-purpose (plain)
  flour
1 teaspoon baking powder
3 tablespoons Dutch cocoa
  powder
2 eggs
1 teaspoon vanilla extract
HOT FUDGE SAUCE
1 cup white sugar
½ cup brown sugar
½ cup cocoa powder
2 tablespoons all-purpose (plain)
  flour
2 tablespoons butter
¼ teaspoon salt
¼ teaspoon vanilla extract

1. Preheat the oven to 300°F (150°C) and butter a 9½in (24cm) non-stick springform cake tin, or small moulds.

2. In a saucepan, melt the butter, then add the chocolate, sugars, brandy and 1½ cups water. Mix well with a whisk until the mixture is smooth.

3. Sift together the flour, baking powder and cocoa and add to the chocolate mixture with the eggs and vanilla. Beat just until combined – don't worry if the mixture is lumpy.

4. Pour into the cake tin and bake for 50 minutes or, if using moulds for 30 minutes. Allow to cool in the tin or moulds for 15 minutes, then turn out.

5. To make hot fudge sauce, mix dry ingredients in a medium saucepan and add butter and ¾ cup water. Bring to the boil and continue boiling for about 10 minutes. Remove from heat and add vanilla extract.

6. Dust with icing sugar and serve warm with cream or ice cream and hot fudge sauce.

Cappucino chocolate cheesecake

serves 8

1.   Preheat oven to 365°F (185°C). Stir together wafer crumbs and cinnamon. Pat into bottom of 8½in (22cm) springform pan.

2.   Beat cream cheese until light and fluffy. Beat in sugar and cocoa powder, then beat in eggs. Stir in 2 cups sour cream, the coffee liqueur and vanilla. Turn into prepared pan and bake for 30 minutes or until set.

3.   Spread remaining sour cream evenly over top. Return to oven for 1 minute. Cool to room temperature, then chill thoroughly, covered. Remove from spring form pan. Just before serving, dust with extra cocoa powder.

1¼ cups chocolate wafers, crushed

⅛ teaspoon ground cinnamon

1 cup light cream cheese

1 cup sugar

1 cup unsweetened cocoa powder

2 eggs

2½ cups sour cream

2 tablespoon coffee liqueur

1 teaspoon vanilla extract

2 tablespoons cocoa powder, for dusting

Torta di cioccolata

1. Preheat the oven to 350°F (180°C) and butter a 7¾in (20cm) non-stick springform tin.

2. Place the butter and chocolate in a heatproof bowl and set over a saucepan of simmering water. Stir gently until the chocolate is thoroughly melted and the mixture is smooth. Whisk in the coffee powder and Dutch cocoa then set aside.

3. In a separate bowl, beat the eggs and sugar together until thick and pale, about 5 minutes. Fold in the ground walnut and walnut pieces.

4. Gently fold together the chocolate mixture and the walnut mixture until thoroughly combined, then pour into the prepared cake tin.

5. Bake for 40 minutes or until the top of the cake is dry. Turn off the oven and leave the cake undisturbed to cool.

6. When cool, take it from the cold oven and gently remove from the tin.

7. Dust with a combination of the cocoa and pure icing sugar and serve in thin slices.

3½oz (100g) butter
12oz (340g) milk chocolate, broken into pieces
1 tablespoon instant coffee powder
3 tablespoons Dutch cocoa powder
5 large eggs
1 cup superfine (caster) sugar
5 tablespoons ground walnuts
3½oz (100g) walnut pieces
1 tablespoon cocoa powder, for dusting
1 tablespoon powdered (icing) sugar, for dusting

cookies

Chocolate raspberry brownies

makes 16

1. Preheat the oven to 350°F (180°C). Butter and line the base and sides of a 11¾ x 7¾in (30 x 20cm) baking tin with baking paper.

2. Sift the flour, baking soda and cocoa into a large bowl and make a well in the centre.

3. Whisk together the eggs, sugar, vanilla, oil and yoghurt in a large jug. Add to the flour mixture and mix until smooth. Fold through the apple purée and raspberries.

4. Spoon the mixture into the prepared tin and bake for 30 minutes or until a skewer comes out clean when inserted in the centre. Allow to cool for 5 minutes in the tin before turning out onto a wire rack to cool completely.

5. Cut into 16 squares and dust with powdered sugar. Serve cool or warm with extra fresh berries and ice cream.

1 cup all-purpose (plain) flour
2 teaspoons baking soda
¾ cup cocoa powder
2 eggs, lightly beaten
1¼ cups superfine (caster) sugar
1 teaspoon vanilla extract
1½ tablespoons sunflower oil
7oz (200g) vanilla yoghurt
½ cup apple purée
7oz (200g) fresh or frozen raspberries
powdered (icing) sugar, for dusting

Double chocolate chip cookies

makes 30

1. Preheat oven to 320°F (160°C).
2. Cream butter and sugars until light and fluffy.
3. Mix in vanilla essence and egg.
4. Stir in flour and cocoa.
5. Add dark chocolate chips.
6. Place teaspoons of mixture on greased baking tray and bake in moderate oven for 10–15 minutes.

4oz (125g) butter
1 cup brown sugar
¾ cup superfine (caster) sugar
1 teaspoon vanilla essence
1 egg
1½ cups self raising flour
½ cup cocoa
¾ cup dark chocolate chips

Chocolate macaroons

makes 20

2 egg whites
¾ cup superfine (caster) sugar
½ cup cocoa powder, sifted
1½ cups shredded coconut

1. Preheat oven to 350°F (180°C). Place egg whites in a bowl and beat until stiff peaks form. Gradually beat in sugar and continue beating until mixture is thick and glossy.

2. Fold cocoa powder and coconut into egg whites. Drop tablespoonfuls of mixture onto buttered baking trays and bake for 15 minutes or until firm. Transfer to wire racks to cool.

NOTE
Avoid baking these on a humid day as moisture will affect their texture. Store macaroons in an airtight container in a cool, dry place.

Double fudge blondies

makes 24

9oz (250g) butter, softened
1½ cups sugar
1 teaspoon vanilla extract
4 eggs, lightly beaten
1¾ cups all-purpose (plain) flour
½ teaspoon baking powder
6oz (185g) white chocolate,
   melted
CREAM CHEESE FILLING
9oz (250g) cream cheese,
   softened
2oz (60g) white chocolate,
   melted
¼ cup maple syrup
1 egg
1 tablespoon all-purpose (plain)
   flour

1. Preheat oven to 350°F (180°C). To make filling, place cream cheese, chocolate, maple syrup, egg and flour in a bowl and beat until smooth. Set aside.
2. Place butter, sugar and vanilla extract in a bowl and beat until light and fluffy. Gradually beat in eggs.
3. Sift together flour and baking powder over butter mixture. Add chocolate and mix well to combine.
4. Spread half the mixture over the base of a buttered and lined 9in (23cm) square cake tin. Top with filling, then remaining mixture. Bake for 40 minutes or until firm. Cool in tin, then cut into squares.

NOTE
These lusciously rich white brownies can double as a dinner party dessert if drizzled with melted white or dark chocolate and topped with toasted flaked almonds.

Choc-filled butterscotch pecan thins

makes 30

1. Using an electric mixer, cream the butter with the sugar until light and fluffy, then beat in the egg and vanilla.

2. Sift in the flour, baking powder and salt and mix until firm enough to handle. Halve the dough then roll each half into a 15cm log. Wrap each log in a piece of cling wrap, using it to help you roll a tight and even log. Chill for 4 hours or overnight.

3. Preheat oven to 350°F (180°C). Cut the logs into 5mm-thick slices with a sharp knife and arrange on lightly buttered baking trays, leaving plenty of room for spreading. Press a pecan half onto each cookie.

4. Bake in batches in the middle of the oven for 10–12 minutes or until golden brown, then cool on the baking trays for 1 minute. Transfer all the biscuits to racks and let them cool.

5. To make the ganache, break the chocolate into small pieces and heat the cream until almost boiling. Pour the hot cream over the chocolate and allow to melt slowly. After 5 minutes, mix until the chocolate has melted and the mixture is thick and smooth.

6. Leave the ganache at room temperature until cool and spreadable. Spoon a small mound of ganache onto half of the biscuits. Gently press another cookie onto the chocolate, to spread the filling. Allow to set, then serve.

13oz (370g) unsalted butter, softened
1 cup firmly packed light brown sugar
1 large egg
1½ teaspoons vanilla extract
1½ cups all-purpose (plain) flour
¾ teaspoon baking powder
½ teaspoon salt
about 60 pecan halves
GANACHE
3½oz (100g) bittersweet chocolate
3½fl oz (100ml) thickened cream

Chocolate raspberry slice

makes 18

1. Preheat oven to 350°F (180°C). Cream butter and sugar, add egg, vanilla and sifted flour. Mix into stiff dough.
2. Roll mixture out and cut to fit a 7–11in (18–28cm) tin, then spread with the raspberry jam.
3. Mix all topping ingredients together and spread over the jam layer.
4. Bake for 15–20 minutes.

½ cup butter
½ cup sugar
1 egg
1 cup self-rising (self-raising) flour
1 teaspoon vanilla extract
1 cup raspberry jam
TOPPING
1 egg
1 cup desiccated coconut
½ cup sugar
3 tablespoons cocoa powder

Original choc chip cookies

makes 35

9oz (250g) butter, softened

1 cup brown sugar

1 egg

1½ cups self-rising (self-raising) flour

½ cup all-purpose (plain) flour

1½oz (45g) desiccated coconut

7¾oz (220g) chocolate chips

6oz (185g) hazelnuts, toasted, and roughly chopped

1. Preheat oven to 350°F (180°C). Place butter and sugar in a bowl and beat until light and fluffy. Beat in egg.

2. Add self-rising flour, all-purpose flour, coconut, chocolate chips and hazelnuts and mix to combine.

3. Drop tablespoonfuls of mixture onto buttered baking trays and bake for 12–15 minutes or until golden. Transfer to wire racks to cool.

White choc hazelnut cookies

makes 24

2 cups chocolate hazelnut spread
4oz (125g) butter, softened
2 cups brown sugar
1 tablespoon vanilla extract
3 eggs, lightly beaten
1¾ cups all-purpose (plain) flour
2 teaspoons baking powder
6oz (185g) hazelnuts, toasted
  and roughly chopped
9oz (250g) white chocolate,
  chopped

1. Preheat oven to 350°F (180°C). Place chocolate hazelnut spread, butter, sugar and vanilla in a bowl and beat until thick and creamy. Gradually beat in eggs.

2. Sift together flour and baking powder. Fold flour mixture into butter mixture. Add hazelnuts and chocolate and mix to combine.

3. Drop tablespoonfuls of mixture onto buttered baking trays and bake for 10 minutes or until golden. Transfer to wire racks to cool.

NOTE
If desired, pipe additional chocolate hazelnut spread in thin lines across the top of these biscuits before serving.

Mocha truffle cookies

makes 40

1. Preheat oven to 350°F (180°C). Place butter, chocolate and coffee powder in a heatproof bowl set over a saucepan of simmering water and heat, stirring, until mixture is smooth. Remove bowl from pan and set aside to cool slightly.

2. Sift together flour, cocoa powder and baking powder into a bowl. Add eggs, sugar, brown sugar, vanilla and chocolate mixture and mix well to combine. Stir in pecans.

3. Drop tablespoonfuls of mixture onto buttered baking trays and bake for 12 minutes or until puffed. Stand on trays for 2 minutes before transferring to wire racks to cool.

NOTE

This is the biscuit version of the traditional rich truffle confection and tastes delicious as an after-dinner treat with coffee.

9oz (250g) butter, chopped
3oz (90g) dark chocolate, broken into pieces
2 tablespoons instant coffee powder
2½ cups all-purpose (plain) flour
½ cup cocoa powder
1 teaspoon baking powder
3 eggs, lightly beaten
1 cup sugar
1 cup brown sugar
2 teaspoons vanilla extract
4oz (125g) pecans, chopped

Choc layer biscuits

makes 40

1. Preheat oven to 350°F (180°C). Place butter, brown sugar, sugar and vanilla in a bowl and beat until light and fluffy. Add egg and beat well. Sift together flour and baking powder. Add flour mixture to butter mixture and mix to make a soft dough.

2. Divide dough into two equal portions. Knead cocoa powder into one portion and malted milk powder into the other.

3. Roll out each portion of dough separately on non-stick baking paper to make two 7¾ x 11¾in (20 x 30cm) rectangles. Place chocolate dough on top of malt dough and press together.

4. Cut in half lengthwise and place one half on top of the other. You should now have four layers of dough in alternating colours. Place layered dough on a tray, cover with cling wrap and chill for 1 hour.

5. Cut dough into ¼in- (1cm) wide fingers and place on buttered baking trays. Bake for 15 minutes or until biscuits are golden and crisp. Transfer to wire racks to cool.

NOTE

For a special occasion, dip the ends of cooled biscuits into melted white or dark chocolate and place on a wire rack until chocolate sets.

9oz (250g) butter, softened
1 cup brown sugar
¾ cup sugar
2 teaspoons vanilla extract
1 egg
2¾ cups all-purpose (plain) flour
1 teaspoon baking powder
½ cups cocoa powder
½ cup malted milk powder

Chocolate snow bombs

makes approx. 32

1½ cup all-purpose (plain) flour
1 cup sugar
½ cup cocoa powder
1 teaspoon baking powder
1 teaspoon salt
2½oz (75g) butter
2 eggs, beaten
¼ teaspoon vanilla extract
1 cup powdered (icing) sugar

1. Preheat oven to 350°F (180°C). Sift the flour, sugar, cocoa, baking powder and salt and rub in the butter. This can be done in a food processor or mixer if desired.

2. Stir in the eggs and vanilla until mixture is blended.

3. Roll dough into small balls and toss well in powdered sugar. Do not dust off excess sugar – the better coated they are the more spectacular the result.

4. Bake for 15 minutes, then cool on a wire rack. Store in an airtight container.

Almond & white chocolate macaroons

serves 10

7oz (200g) marzipan
1 cup superfine (caster) sugar
2 large egg whites
½ cup toasted, flaked almonds
¼ cup thickened cream
1½oz (45g) unsalted butter
grated zest of 1 orange
6oz (170g) white chocolate,
　chopped
1 tablespoon powdered (icing)
　sugar, for dusting

1. Preheat the oven to 350°F (175°C). Generously butter two large non-stick baking trays and set aside.

2. Process the marzipan, sugar and egg whites in the processor until smooth and thick, then spoon tablespoonful of the mixture onto prepared trays, making the mixture into finger-size lengths rather than rounds. Leave space around each biscuit. Sprinkle some almonds onto each biscuit, then bake for 10 minutes or until golden brown. Let the biscuits cool on the trays for 5 minutes after baking then, using a spatula, transfer the biscuits to a rack and cool completely.

3. To make the filling, bring the cream, butter and orange zest to a simmer in a small saucepan, then add the chocolate and stir until smooth. Remove from the heat and let the filling cool until thick but spreadable, about 15 minutes.

4. When the biscuits are completely cold, spread some chocolate filling over the flat side of one, then sandwich with another one. Repeat with the remaining biscuits and filling. Store in an airtight container. Dust with a little icing sugar before serving.

small delights

Hazelnut snowballs

makes 40

1. Place chocolate, butter, cream and liqueur in a heatproof bowl set over a saucepan of simmering water and heat, stirring, until mixture is smooth. Remove bowl from pan and set aside to cool slightly.
2. Stir chocolate mixture until thick and pliable. Roll tablespoonfuls of mixture into balls. Press a hazelnut into the centre of each ball and roll to enclose. Roll balls in coconut and refrigerate for 1 hour or until firm.

7oz (200g) white chocolate, broken into pieces
1½oz (45g) butter, chopped
¼ cup double cream
1 tablespoon hazelnut-flavoured liqueur
4oz (125g) hazelnuts, toasted and skins removed
2oz (60g) desiccated coconut

Chocolate fig truffles

makes 24

1. Place chocolate, butter, cream, golden syrup and cognac or brandy in a heatproof bowl set over a saucepan of simmering water and heat, stirring, until smooth. Remove bowl from pan.

2. Add figs and slivered almonds to chocolate mixture and mix well to combine. Chill mixture for 1 hour or until firm enough to roll into balls.

3. Take 3 teaspoonfuls of mixture and roll into balls, then roll in flaked almonds. Place on non-stick baking paper and chill until required.

NOTE
If preferred, chopped prunes or dates may be used in place of the figs.

6oz (185g) milk chocolate, broken into pieces
3oz (90g) butter, chopped
½ cup double cream
¼ cup golden syrup
1 tablespoon cognac or brandy
2½oz (75g) dried figs, chopped
1½oz (45g) slivered almonds, toasted
2oz (60g) flaked almonds, toasted

Tiny fudge cakes

makes 20

3½oz (100g) dark chocolate
2oz (60g) butter
3 eggs, separated
½ cup superfine (caster) sugar
¼ cup all-purpose (plain) flour,
  sifted
sugared violets, optional
WHITE CHOCOLATE
  FROSTING
3½oz (100g) white chocolate,
  chopped
2 tablespoons double cream

1. Preheat oven to 350°F (180°C). Place dark chocolate and butter in a heatproof bowl set over a saucepan of simmering water and heat, stirring, until smooth. Remove bowl from pan and set aside to cool slightly.

2. Place egg yolks and sugar in a bowl and beat until thick and pale. Fold flour into egg mixture. Add chocolate mixture and mix to combine.

3. Place egg whites into a clean bowl and beat until stiff peaks form. Fold egg whites into chocolate mixture.

4. Spoon mixture into buttered mini cupcake tins or small paper cupcake cases and bake for 10 minutes. Remove from tins and cool on wire racks.

5. To make frosting, place white chocolate and cream in a heatproof bowl set over a saucepan of simmering water and heat, stirring, until smooth. Remove bowl from pan and set aside until mixture thickens slightly. Spread frosting over cakes and decorate with sugared violets.

NOTE
Sugared violets are available from cake decorators' suppliers and specialty kitchen shops.

Marbled shells

makes 30

7oz (200g) dark chocolate,
  melted
7oz (200g) white chocolate,
  melted
CREAMY CHOCOLATE
  FILLING
7oz (200g) milk chocolate
½ cup double cream
2 tablespoons coffee or hazelnut-
  flavoured liqueur

1. To make filling, place milk chocolate, cream and liqueur in a heatproof bowl set over a saucepan of simmering water and heat, stirring, until mixture is smooth. Remove bowl from pan and set aside until mixture cools and thickens.

2. Place a teaspoonful of dark chocolate and a teaspoonful of white chocolate in a shell-shaped chocolate mould. Swirl with a skewer to marble chocolate and, using a small brush, brush chocolate evenly over mould. Tap mould gently on work surface to remove any air bubbles. Repeat with remaining chocolate to make 30 moulds. Freeze for 2 minutes or until chocolate sets.

3. Place a small spoonful of filling in each chocolate shell. Spoon equal quantities of the remaining dark and white chocolate over filling to fill mould. Using a skewer, carefully swirl chocolate to give marbled effect. Tap mould gently on work surface. Freeze for 3 minutes or until chocolate sets. Tap moulds gently to remove chocolates.

NOTE
Do not overmix the white and dark chocolates or the marbled effect will diminish. Make sure the first coating sets completely before adding the filling so that the first coating does not crack.

Tuile cups with white chocolate

makes 28

1. Preheat oven to 320°F (160°C). Place butter, egg whites, milk, flour and sugar in a bowl and beat until smooth.

2. Place 2 teaspoonfuls of mixture on a lightly buttered baking tray and spread out to make a 10cm round. Repeat leaving 10cm between each tuile. Sprinkle with almonds and bake for 3–5 minutes or until edges are golden. Bake only two or three tuiles at a time and work quickly, as each cup must be shaped before the biscuit cools.

3. Using a spatula, carefully remove tuiles from trays and place over a small upturned strainer. Press gently to shape, then allow to cool and harden before removing from strainer. Repeat with remaining mixture.

4. To make filling, place chocolate, butter and cream in a heatproof bowl set over a saucepan of simmering water and heat, stirring, until smooth. Remove bowl from pan and set aside until mixture thickens slightly. Beat mixture until light and thick. Spoon mixture into a piping bag (see page 17) and pipe into tuile cups.

4oz (125g) butter, melted
4 egg whites
2 tablespoons milk
1 cup all-purpose (plain) flour
⅔ cup superfine (caster) sugar
2oz (60g) flaked almonds
WHITE CHOCOLATE
  FILLING
9oz (250g) white chocolate,
  broken into pieces
2oz (60g) butter, chopped
¼ cup double cream

Chocolate nougat hearts

makes 40

1. Place chocolate, butter and cream in a heatproof bowl set over a saucepan of simmering water and heat, stirring, until mixture is smooth.

2. Add nougat and almonds and mix well to combine. Pour mixture into a buttered and lined 7 x 11in (18 x 28cm) shallow cake tin. Refrigerate for 2 hours or until set.

3. Using a heart-shaped cutter, cut out hearts from set mixture.

NOTE
Dip cutter into warm water and dry on a clean towel between each cut to achieve neat, straight edges.

13oz (375g) milk chocolate,
  broken into pieces
1½oz (45g) butter, chopped
¼ cup double cream
7oz (200g) nougat, chopped
3½oz (100g) almonds, toasted
  and chopped

Chocolate almond balls

makes 24

½ cup thickened cream
4oz (120g) bittersweet chocolate,
    chopped
½oz (15g) butter
2oz (60g) toasted almonds, finely
    chopped
1oz (30g) puffed rice cereal,
    crushed

1. Place the cream and chocolate in a saucepan and cook over a low heat, stirring, until the chocolate melts. Remove the pan from the heat and set aside to cool slightly. Stir in the butter, cover and chill in refrigerator.

2. Using an electric mixer, beat the chocolate mixture until soft peaks form. Return to the refrigerator until firm.

3. Place the almonds and rice cereal in a bowl and mix to combine. Shape teaspoonfuls of the chocolate mixture into balls and roll in the almond mixture. Store in an airtight container in the refrigerator.

NOTE
Served with coffee, this uncooked biscuit makes a delicious after-dinner treat.

Chocolate panforte

makes 32

1 cup liquid honey

1 cup sugar

9oz (250g) almonds, toasted and chopped

9oz (250g) hazelnuts, toasted and chopped

4oz (125g) glacé apricots, chopped

4oz (125g) glacé peaches, chopped

3½oz (100g) candied mixed peel

1¼ cups all-purpose (plain) flour, sifted

¼ cup cocoa powder, sifted

2 teaspoons ground cinnamon

5½oz (155g) dark chocolate, melted

rice paper

1. Preheat oven to 400°F (200°C). Place honey and sugar in a small saucepan and heat, stirring constantly, over a low heat until sugar dissolves. Bring to the boil, then reduce heat and simmer, stirring constantly, for 5 minutes or until mixture thickens.

2. Place almonds, hazelnuts, apricots, peaches, mixed peel, flour, cocoa powder and cinnamon in a bowl and mix to combine. Stir in honey syrup. Add chocolate and mix well to combine.

3. Line an 7 x 11in (18 x 28cm) shallow cake tin with rice paper. Pour mixture into tin and bake for 20 minutes. Turn onto a wire rack to cool, then cut into small pieces.

Pistachio truffles

makes 40

1. Place chocolate, butter, cream and sugar in a heatproof bowl set over a saucepan of simmering water and heat, stirring, until smooth. Add liqueur and half the pistachios and mix well to combine. Chill for 1 hour or until firm enough to roll into balls.

2. Roll tablespoonfuls of mixture into balls, then roll in remaining pistachios. Chill until required.

NOTE
To bring out the lovely green colour of the pistachios, blanch the shelled nuts in boiling water for 30 seconds, drain and vigorously rub in a clean towel to remove their skins.

11oz (320g) dark chocolate,
   broken into pieces
1½oz (45g) butter, chopped
½ cup double cream
2 tablespoons sugar
2 tablespoons Galliano
4oz (125g) pistachios, chopped

Caramel walnut petits fours

makes 40

1. Place sugar, brown sugar, cream, golden syrup and butter in a saucepan and heat over a low heat, stirring constantly, until sugar dissolves. As sugar crystals form on sides of pan, brush with a wet pastry brush.

2. Bring syrup to the boil and stir in baking soda. Reduce heat and simmer until syrup reaches the hard ball stage or 250°F (120°C) on a sugar thermometer.

3. Stir in walnuts and vanilla and pour mixture into a buttered and foil-lined 7¾in (20cm) square cake tin. Set aside at room temperature for 5 hours or until caramel sets.

4. Remove caramel from tin and cut into 2cm squares.

5. To make frosting, combine chocolate and oil. Half-dip caramels in melted chocolate, place on baking paper and leave to set.

NOTE

For easy removal of the caramel from the tin, allow the foil lining to overhang the tin on two opposite sides to form handles.

1 cup sugar
½ cup brown sugar
2 cups double cream
1 cup golden syrup
2oz (60g) butter, chopped
½ teaspoon baking soda
5oz (150g) walnuts, chopped
1 tablespoon vanilla extract
CHOCOLATE FROSTING
13oz (375g) dark or milk
  chocolate, melted
2 teaspoons vegetable oil

Chocolate flapjacks

makes 10–12

7¾oz (220g) butter
1 cup raw sugar
¼ cup golden syrup
3 tablespoons cocoa powder
3½ cups rolled oats
3½oz (100g) dark chocolate melts

1. Preheat oven to 375°F (190°C). Melt butter, sugar and golden syrup in a saucepan large enough to mix all the ingredients. Mix in cocoa. Remove from heat and mix in rolled oats.

2. Press into a 11 x 7in (28 x 18cm) shallow tin with a baking-paper-lined base. Bake for 30–35 minutes or until cooked.

3. Cool for 5 minutes before marking flapjacks into squares or fingers.

4. Melt chocolate. Drizzle over flapjacks and leave to set. Cut flapjacks through completely when cold.

Melted chocolate pecan brownies

makes 12

7oz (200g) dark cooking
  chocolate
3½oz (100g) butter
1½ cups white sugar
4 eggs
1 cup all-purpose (plain) flour
½ teaspoon baking powder
1 teaspoon vanilla extract
¼ cup pecans, chopped

1. Preheat oven to 375°F (190°C). Melt chocolate and butter together in a saucepan over a medium heat.

2. Remove from heat, stir in sugar and cool slightly. Add eggs and beat with a wooden spoon to combine. Mix in flour, baking powder and vanilla until smooth. Mix in pecans.

3. Pour into a 7¾in (20cm) square cake tin lined with baking paper. Bake for 30–35 minutes or until set. Cut into squares to serve.

Banana mousse

1. Place gelatine and ¼ cup boiling water in a bowl and stir until gelatine dissolves. Set aside to cool.

2. Place bananas, sugar and lemon juice in a food processor and process until smooth. Stir gelatine mixture into banana mixture.

3. Place cream and coconut milk in a bowl and beat until soft peaks form. Fold cream mixture into banana mixture.

4. Spoon mousse into six serving glasses. Divide melted chocolate between glasses and swirl with a skewer. Refrigerate for 2 hours or until set.

NOTE
Dried banana chips make an attractive garnish with fresh mint leaves.

1 tablespoon gelatine
17½oz (500g) ripe bananas
¼ cup sugar
1 tablespoon lemon juice
1 cup double cream
3½fl oz (100ml) coconut milk
3½oz (100g) dark chocolate, melted

Baked fudge with rum sauce

serves 8

1. Preheat oven to 350°F (180°C). Mix sugar, flour and cocoa. Add to beaten eggs and blend thoroughly. Melt butter and add vanilla. Thoroughly combine butter and cocoa mixtures. Add nuts.

2. Bake in individual custard cups in a pan of hot water for 45 minutes to 1 hour. The fudge should be firm, like custard.

3. For sauce, mix together egg yolk, sugar and rum. Fold this mixture into stiffly whipped cream. Serve on top of slightly warm baked fudge.

2¼ cups sugar
⅔ cup all-purpose (plain) flour
⅔ cup cocoa powder
5 eggs, well beaten
7oz (200g) butter
2 teaspoons vanilla extract
1 cup pecans, coarsely chopped
SAUCE
1 egg yolk
½ cup powdered (icing) sugar, sifted
3 tablespoons light rum
1 cup thickened cream, whipped

Five-minute chocolate cake

serves 1

4 tablespoons all-purpose (plain)
  flour
4 tablespoons sugar
2 tablespoons cocoa
1 egg
3 tablespoons milk
3 tablespoons olive oil
3 tablespoons chocolate chips
a small splash of vanilla extract

1. Add flour, sugar and cocoa to a microwave proof mug, and mix well. Add the egg and mix thoroughly. Pour in the milk and oil and mix well. Add the chocolate chips and vanilla, and mix again.

2. Put the mug in the microwave and cook for 3 minutes at full power. The cake will rise over the top of the mug, something like a souffle. Allow to cool a little, and tip out onto a plate if desired, or eat with a spoon directly from the mug.

Banana choc chip soufflés

serves 6

3 large egg whites

⅓ cup sugar

2 firm, ripe bananas, about 6oz (170g) each

2½ tablespoons semisweet chocolate chips

1. Preheat oven to 430°F (220°C) and lightly butter six ¾-cup ramekins.

2. Beat egg whites until they just hold soft peaks, then gradually beat in sugar until meringue holds stiff peaks. Coarsely grate bananas onto meringue and gently fold chocolate chips into meringue.

3. Arrange ramekins on a baking sheet and divide mixture evenly among them. Run a knife around sides of ramekins, freeing mixture to aid rising, and bake soufflés in middle of oven until puffed and golden brown, about 15 minutes. Serve immediately.

special occasion

Chocolate crème brûlée

serves 12

1. Preheat oven to 300°F (150°C). Cut the plum pudding into tiny cubes and sprinkle equally over the bases of 12 ovenproof ramekins.

2. Place a large stainless steel bowl over a pot of simmering water, add the cream and sugar and whisk together gently until the sugar has dissolved. Add the chocolate, broken into small pieces, and continue mixing until the chocolate has dissolved. Remove from the heat.

3. In a separate bowl, whisk the egg yolks until they form a smooth ribbon. Mix the whisked egg yolks, chocolate mixture and Dutch cocoa until thoroughly combined. Pour this custard mixture into a jug and divide between the prepared ramekins.

4. Place the ramekins into a large ovenproof baking dish and add hot water to reach halfway up the outsides. Bake for 30 minutes or until set. Remove the baking dish and take the ramekins out of the water bath. Chill the custards for at least 2 hours, or overnight.

5. Before serving, sieve the powdered sugar generously over the custards. Caramelise the sugar under a grill until bubbling and golden. Alternatively, you can buy a small blow-torch from a good kitchenware shop and use this to caramelise the sugar. If grilling, watch carefully to avoid burning the sugar.

17½oz (500g) plum pudding
4½ cups thickened cream
3½oz (100g) superfine (caster) sugar
9oz (250g) bittersweet chocolate
8 large egg yolks
1 tablespoon Dutch cocoa powder
3½oz (100g) powdered (icing) sugar, sifted

Chocolate gold

serves 12

1. Preheat oven to 320°F (160°C). Place chocolate and butter in a heatproof bowl set over a saucepan of simmering water and heat, stirring, until smooth. Remove bowl from pan and set aside to cool.

2. Place egg yolks and sugar in a bowl and beat until thick and pale. Fold flour and chocolate mixture into egg yolk mixture. Place egg whites in a clean bowl and beat until stiff peaks form. Fold egg whites into chocolate mixture.

3. Pour mixture into a buttered and lined 9in (23cm) springform tin and bake for 30 minutes or until cake is cooked when tested with a skewer. Cool in tin.

4. To make glaze, place chocolate in a heatproof bowl set over a saucepan of simmering water and heat, stirring, until chocolate melts and is smooth. Stir in oil and mix until combined.

5. Remove cake from tin and place on a wire rack. Pour glaze over cake and allow it to run over sides. Leave to set. Decorate with gold leaf and serve with cream.

6. note The bottom of a baked cake is often smoother than the top so, to ensure a perfectly smooth surface for glazing, invert the cooled cake onto another springform base or a 9in (23cm) circle of foil-covered cardboard.

9oz (250g) dark chocolate, broken into pieces
5½oz (160g) butter, chopped
4 eggs, separated
¾ cup sugar
⅓ cup all-purpose (plain) flour, sifted
gold leaf
CHOCOLATE MIRROR GLAZE
9oz (250g) dark chocolate, broken into pieces
3 teaspoons vegetable oil

Hearts of chocolate

serves 10

1 quantity Simple Chocolate
Cake mix (see page 50)
½ cup cocoa powder, sifted
white chocolate curls (see
page 14)
dark chocolate curls (see
page 14)
CREAMY CHOCOLATE
FILLING
13oz (375g) milk chocolate,
broken into pieces
5½oz (160g) butter, chopped
¾ cup double cream

1. Preheat oven to 375°F (190°C). Prepare Simple Chocolate Cake mix, following steps 1 and 2 on page 50. Pour mixture into a buttered and base-lined heart-shaped cake tin and bake for 40 minutes or until cooked when tested with a skewer. Stand cake in tin for 5 minutes. Turn onto a wire rack to cool.

2. Trim top of cake and turn upside down. Scoop out centre of cake, leaving a ¾in (2cm) border. Do not cut right the way through the cake, but leave ¾in (2cm) of cake to form the base.

3. To make filling, place chocolate, butter and cream in a heatproof bowl set over a saucepan of simmering water and heat, stirring, until smooth. Remove bowl from pan and set aside to cool. Beat until light and creamy. Pour filling into prepared cake and chill for 4 hours or until filling is firm. Place cake on a serving plate. Dust top with cocoa powder and decorate with chocolate curls.

Pink & white mousse

serves 8

17½oz (500g) mixed berries
1 cup sugar
1 tablespoon orange-flavoured
   liqueur
6 egg yolks
7oz (200g) white chocolate,
   melted
2 teaspoons vanilla extract
1⅔ cup double cream, whipped
white chocolate curls (see
   page 14)

1. Place berries in a food processor or blender and process to make a purée. Press purée through a sieve into a saucepan. Stir in ⅓ cup sugar and the liqueur and bring to simmering over a low heat. Simmer, stirring occasionally, until mixture reduces to 1 cup. Remove pan from heat and set aside.

2. Place ¼ cup water, the egg yolks and remaining sugar in a heatproof bowl set over a saucepan of simmering water and beat for 8 minutes or until mixture is light and creamy. Remove bowl from pan. Add chocolate and vanilla and beat until mixture cools. Fold whipped cream into chocolate mixture. Divide mixture into two portions.

3. Stir berry purée into one portion of mixture and leave one portion plain. Drop alternate spoonfuls of berry and plain mixtures into serving glasses. Using a skewer, swirl mixtures to give a ripple effect. Refrigerate until firm. Just prior to serving, decorate with chocolate curls.

NOTE
Garnish with additional fresh berries or red and white currants when available.

Triple mousse cake

serves 12

1. Using a serrated knife, cut sponge horizontally into three even layers and place one layer in base of a lined 9in (23cm) springform tin.

2. To make chocolate mousse, place dark chocolate, brandy and egg yolk in a bowl and mix until smooth. Place egg whites in a clean bowl and beat until soft peaks form. Gradually beat in sugar and continue beating until stiff peaks form. Fold chocolate mixture and cream into egg whites. Pour mousse over sponge and chill for 1 hour or until mousse is firm. Top with a second layer of sponge.

3. To make mocha mousse, place milk chocolate, coffee and egg yolk in a bowl and mix until smooth. Place egg whites in a clean bowl and beat until soft peaks form. Gradually beat in sugar and continue beating until stiff peaks form. Fold chocolate mixture and cream into egg whites. Pour mousse over sponge and chill for 1 hour or until firm. Top with remaining sponge layer.

4. To make white chocolate mousse, place white chocolate and 2 tablespoons water in a heatproof bowl set over a saucepan of simmering water and heat, stirring, until smooth. Remove bowl from pan and set aside to cool slightly. Fold chocolate mixture into cream, then pour over sponge. Chill for 3 hours or until firm then decorate with chocolate curls.

9in (23cm) sponge cake
chocolate curls (see page 14)
CHOCOLATE MOUSSE
6oz (185g) dark chocolate,
  melted
2 tablespoons brandy
1 egg yolk
2 egg whites
1 tablespoon sugar
⅓ cup double cream, whipped
MOCHA MOUSSE
6oz (185g) milk chocolate
2 tablespoons strong black coffee
1 egg yolk
2 egg whites
1 tablespoon sugar
⅓ cup double cream, whipped
WHITE CHOCOLATE
  MOUSSE
6oz (185g) white chocolate
1 cup double cream, whipped

Black & white tart

1. Preheat oven to 350°F (180°C). Beat egg whites in a bowl until soft peaks form. Gradually beat in sugar. Fold in coconut and flour. Press mixture over base and up sides of a buttered and lined 9in (23cm) springform flan tin. Bake for 20–25 minutes or until golden. Stand in tin for 5 minutes then remove and cool on a wire rack.

2. To make filling, place egg yolks and cream in a heatproof bowl set over a saucepan of simmering water and beat until thick and pale. Stir in dark chocolate and cognac or brandy and continue stirring until chocolate melts. Remove bowl from pan and set aside to cool.

3. Place white chocolate and sour cream in a heatproof bowl over a saucepan of simmering water and heat, stirring, until smooth. Remove bowl from pan and set aside to cool.

4. Place alternating spoonfuls of dark and white mixtures in macaroon shell and, using a skewer, swirl to give a marbled effect. Chill for 2 hours or until filling is firm.

5. To make coulis, place raspberries in a food processor and process to make a purée. Press purée through a sieve to remove seeds, then stir in sugar. Serve with tart.

NOTE
This dessert is best served the day it is made as the macaroon shell may absorb too much moisture on standing and lose its crispness.

2 egg whites
½ cup superfine (caster) sugar
7¾oz (220g) desiccated coconut
¼ cup all-purpose (plain) flour, sifted
CHOCOLATE SOUR CREAM FILLING
2 egg yolks
¾ cup double cream
6oz (185g) dark chocolate
2 tablespoons cognac or brandy
6oz (185g) white chocolate
⅔ cup sour cream
RASPBERRY COULIS
9oz (250g) raspberries
1 tablespoon powdered (icing) sugar, sifted

Chocolate mascarpone roulade

serves 8–10

6oz (185g) dark chocolate
¼ cup strong black coffee
5 eggs, separated
½ cup superfine (caster) sugar
2 tablespoons self-rising (self-raising) flour, sifted
½ cup chocolate hazelnut spread
frosted rose petals
MASCARPONE FILLING
13oz (375g) mascarpone
2 tablespoons powdered (icing) sugar, sifted
2 tablespoons brandy

1. Preheat oven to 320°F (160°C). Place chocolate and coffee in a heatproof bowl set over a saucepan of simmering water and heat, stirring, until smooth. Cool slightly.
2. Beat egg yolks until thick and pale. Gradually beat in superfine sugar. Fold chocolate mixture and flour into egg yolks.
3. Beat egg whites until stiff peaks form. Fold into chocolate mixture. Pour mixture into a buttered and lined 10 x 1in (26 x 3cm) Swiss roll tin and bake for 20 minutes or until firm. Cool in tin.
4. To make filling, beat mascarpone, powdered sugar and brandy in a bowl.
5. Turn cakes onto a clean tea towel sprinkled with superfine sugar. Spread with chocolate hazelnut spread and half the filling and roll up. Spread with remaining filling and decorate with frosted rose petals.

NOTE
To make frosted rose petals, lightly whisk egg white in a shallow bowl and dip in fresh, dry petals to lightly cover. Dip petals in superfine sugar, shake off excess and stand on baking paper to harden.

Chocolate boxes

makes 8

17½oz (500g) pound madeira or
  light fruit cake
7oz (200g) dark chocolate,
  broken
1¼ cups thickened cream,
  whipped
8 strawberries
SYRUP
¼ cup sugar
1 strip lemon or orange zest
3 teaspoons rum or liqueur

1. Even off the top of the cake and cut lengthwise down the centre, then crosswise into 4, making 8 cubes of cake. Place on a wire rack over a tray.

2. Simmer the syrup ingredients together with 1 cup water for 8–10 minutes, then remove the zest. Spoon the syrup over each cake cube until sufficient syrup has been absorbed.

3. Place chocolate in a bowl over simmering water and stir gently as the chocolate melts. Leave strawberries on stem. Dip half the strawberry into the melted chocolate and place on a sheet of baking paper until set.

4. Take 2 pieces of baking paper and mark a 10in (25cm) square on each. Spread the chocolate in a thin layer using a pallet knife or spatula to cover each square. Allow to set.

5. Trim the edges of each square and cut into 5 rows, 5cm wide. Cut each row into 1½in-(4cm) wide pieces giving 20 pieces 1½ x 2in (4 x 5cm) each from each square. You will then have a few spares in case of breakages.

6. Using a round-bladed knife, spread whipped cream onto the rough side of a chocolate square and press onto the side of a cake cube. Repeat with the 3 remaining sides to form a chocolate box.

7. When all 8 boxes are assembled, pipe a rosette of cream into the top recess. Garnish with a chocolate-dipped strawberry.

Chocolate puddings with ginger cream

serves 6

1. Butter 2¼ x 4in (6 x 10cm) ovenproof soufflé dishes. Refrigerate dishes for 20 minutes. Melt the chocolate in a bowl over simmering water. Stir until melted, then stir in the ginger and vanilla.

2. Preheat the oven 375°F (190°C). Remove the soufflé dishes from the refrigerator and butter again. Whisk the egg yolks into the chocolate mixture, then fold in the sugar and flour with a metal spoon. Whisk the egg whites until stiff. Fold a spoonful into the mixture to loosen it, then fold in the remainder. Spoon the mixture into the dishes and cook for 20 minutes or until well risen.

3. Meanwhile, to make the ginger cream, whip the cream until it forms soft peaks. Fold in the ginger cordial and ground ginger and sweeten to taste with powdered sugar. Dust the puddings with powdered sugar and serve warm with the ginger cream.

7oz (200g) milk chocolate, broken into pieces
1 teaspoon ground ginger
1 teaspoon vanilla extract
4 large eggs, separated
5oz (145g) superfine (caster) sugar
2 tablespoons self-rising (self-raising) flour
½ cup powdered (icing) sugar, sifted

GINGER CREAM
1 cup thickened cream
1 tablespoon chilled ginger cordial
1 teaspoon ground ginger
¼ cup powdered (icing) sugar, sifted

Cassata layers

serves 10

1. To make filling place ice cream, cream, apricots, pineapple, cherries, raisins, chocolate and pistachios in a bowl and mix to combine.

2. Split sponge horizontally into three even layers. Place one layer of sponge in the base of a lined 7¾in (20cm) springform tin and sprinkle with 1 tablespoon of liqueur. Top with one-third of the filling. Repeat layers to use all ingredients, ending with a layer of filling. Freeze for 5 hours or until firm. Remove from freezer 1 hour before serving and place in refrigerator.

3. Just prior to serving, decorate with chocolate curls.

NOTE
Use the best quality ice cream you can afford. To retain maximum volume and creamy texture, keep the cassata filling mixture well chilled until the cassata is finally assembled.

7¾in (20cm) sponge cake
¼ cup almond-flavoured liqueur
chocolate curls (see page 14)
CASSATA FILLING
36fl oz (1L) vanilla ice cream,
  softened
1 cup double cream
4oz (125g) glacé apricots,
  chopped
4oz (125g) glacé pineapple,
  chopped
2oz (60g) glacé cherries, chopped
2oz (60g) raisins, halved
4oz (125g) dark chocolate, grated
4oz (125g) pistachios, chopped

Frozen maple nut parfait

serves 8

6 egg yolks
1 cup superfine (caster) sugar
½ cup maple syrup
2½ cups double cream
3½oz (100g) macadamias, finely
    chopped
3½oz (100g) white chocolate,
    chopped

1. Place egg yolks in a bowl and beat until thick and pale. Place sugar and ½ cup water in a saucepan and heat over a low heat, stirring, until sugar dissolves. Bring to the boil and boil until mixture thickens and reaches soft ball stage or 245°F (118°C) on a sugar thermometer.

2. Gradually beat sugar mixture and maple syrup into egg yolks and continue beating until mixture cools. Place cream in a bowl and beat until soft peaks form. Fold cream, macadamias and chocolate into egg mixture.

3. Pour mixture into an aluminium foil-lined 6 x 9¾in (15 x 25cm) loaf tin and freeze for 5 hours or until firm.

4. Turn parfait onto a serving plate, remove foil, cut into slices and drizzle with extra maple syrup.

NOTE
This light and luscious frozen Italian meringue is the perfect partner for a garnish of fresh fruit and perhaps some almond-flavoured biscotti.

Christmas fudge pecan pie

serves 6

2½ cups chocolate wafer crumbs
2oz (60g) butter, melted, plus
  3oz (90g) softened
¾ cup brown sugar
3 eggs
1½ cups semisweet chocolate
  buttons, melted
2 teaspoons instant coffee
1 teaspoon vanilla extract
½ cup flour
1 cup pecans, coarsely chopped
½ cup cream, whipped
morello cherries, optional

1. Preheat oven to 350°F (180°C). Combine chocolate wafer crumbs and $1/3$ cup melted butter; firmly press on bottom and sides of a 8½in (22cm) tart pan or pie plate. Bake for 6–8 minutes.

2. Cream the softened butter. Gradually add brown sugar with the electric mixer at medium speed until blended. Add the eggs one at a time, beating after each addition. Stir in the melted chocolate, instant coffee, vanilla, flour and chopped pecans.

3. Pour into the prepared crust. Bake at 365°F (185°C) for 25 minutes. Remove from oven and cool completely on a rack.

4. Serve with whipped cream with morello cherries stirred through.

Vanilla tiramisu

serves 8

1. Cut the vanilla pod in half and scrape out the seeds.

2. Combine the egg yolks, sugar and cream cheese in a mixing bowl. Beat together with an electric beater until light. Add the mascarpone and vanilla pods and stir to combine.

3. In a separate bowl, beat the egg whites together until soft peaks form. Fold the egg whites into the cream mixture.

4. Mix the coffee and liqueur together in a shallow dish. Dip each biscuit in the coffee mixture.

5. Place half the biscuits in a 7¾in (20cm) dish. Spoon over half the cream mixture and top with the remaining biscuits and cream mixture.

6. Garnish with grated chocolate. Cover and refrigerate for 2 hours or overnight.

NOTE

Tiramisu is best made the day before. It is best to use eggs at room temperature, so remove the eggs from the refrigerator 3 hours before preparation.

1 vanilla pod
2 eggs, separated
½ cup superfine sugar
1 cup cream cheese
1 cup mascarpone
1 cup strong black coffee, cooled
¼ cup coffee-flavoured liqueur
22 Savoiardi sponge biscuits
1¾oz (50g) milk chocolate,
   grated

New York chocolate cake

serves 12

1. Preheat the oven to 350°F (180°C) and butter a 9½in (24cm) non-stick cake tin or long non-stick loaf tin (not springform). Chop the chocolate and place in a large heatproof bowl.

2. In a small saucepan, bring the butter, espresso and brown sugar to the boil and simmer briefly. Pour the liquid over the chopped chocolate and allow to sit for a few minutes. Stir the ingredients gently to help the chocolate melt. Beat the eggs, then add to the chocolate mixture, whisking thoroughly.

3. Pour into the prepared cake tin, then place the tin in a large roasting pan or baking dish. Pour hot (not boiling) water into the roasting pan to reach halfway up the sides of the cake tin, then bake for 1 hour. Remove the cake from the water bath and chill overnight.

4. To make the raspberry sauce, purée the berries and their juice (if using frozen berries, thaw them first) with the lemon juice and sugar. Pour the sauce through a sieve then chill for up to 2 days.

5. The next day, remove the cake from the tin. If this is difficult, fill the kitchen sink with about 1½in (4cm) of boiling water and dip the cake tin base in the water for a few seconds to loosen the cake. Run a knife or spatula around the tin then invert the cake onto a platter. Serve the cake with raspberry sauce and fresh raspberries.

15oz (450g) dark or bittersweet chocolate
15oz (450g) butter
1 cup espresso coffee
1 cup packed brown sugar
8 large eggs
32oz (900g) fresh or frozen raspberries
juice of 1 lemon
2 tablespoons sugar
9oz (250g) fresh raspberries

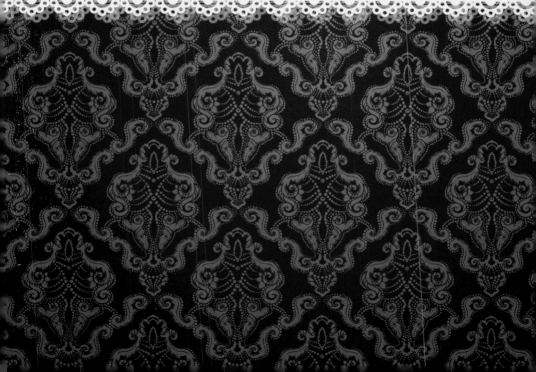

festive

Yule log

serves 8

1. Preheat oven to 350°F (180°C). Place egg yolks and sugar in a bowl and beat until thick and pale. Stir in chocolate, flour and cocoa powder.

2. Place egg whites in a clean bowl and beat until stiff peaks form. Fold egg whites into chocolate mixture.

3. Pour mixture into a buttered and lined 10 x 13in (26 x 32cm) Swiss roll tin and bake for 15 minutes or until firm. Turn cake onto a tea towel sprinkled with superfine sugar and roll up to make a long roll. Set aside to cool.

4. To make filling, place white chocolate in a heatproof bowl set over a saucepan of simmering water and heat, stirring, until smooth. Add cream and stir until combined. Cover and chill until thickened and spreadable.

5. Unroll cake and spread with filling, leaving a 1cm border. Re-roll cake.

6. To make icing, combine melted chocolate and butter and mix until combined. Spread icing over roll, then use a fork to roughly texture the icing.

NOTE
Keep this dessert refrigerated until time to serve. You can dust log with pure icing sugar to create a look of fallen snow just before serving.

5 eggs, separated
¼ cup superfine (caster) sugar
3½oz (100g) dark chocolate, melted and cooled
2 tablespoons self-rising (self-raising) flour, sifted
2 tablespoons cocoa powder, sifted

WHITE CHOCOLATE FILLING
2oz (60g) white chocolate
⅔ cup thickened cream

CHOCOLATE FROSTING
7oz (200g) dark chocolate, melted
2oz (60g) butter, melted

Fruit & nut wreath

serves 8

1. Place sugar and ¾ cup water in a saucepan and heat over a low heat, stirring, until sugar dissolves. Bring to the boil, then reduce heat and simmer for 6 minutes or until syrup is golden.

2. Remove pan from heat and carefully stir in cream. Return pan to heat and cook, stirring, until mixture is smooth.

3. Place nuts, apricots, raisins, pineapple and cherries in a heatproof bowl. Pour caramel over fruit mixture and mix well to combine. Pour mixture into a buttered and lined 7¾in (20cm) ring tin. Allow to set.

4. Remove wreath from tin and drizzle with melted chocolate.

NOTE

This delicious treat makes a beautiful holiday gift when presented in a see-through box wrapped with a green or red satin ribbon.

1¼ cups sugar
¾ cup double cream
11oz (320g) roasted unsalted mixed nuts
4oz (125g) dried apricots
3oz (90g) raisins
4oz (125g) glacé pineapple, chopped
4oz (125g) glacé cherries
4oz (125g) dark chocolate, melted

Ice cream christmas pudding

serves 8

36fl oz (1L) chocolate ice cream,
  softened
4oz (125g) glacé apricots,
  chopped
4oz (125g) glacé cherries,
  chopped
4oz (125g) glacé pears, chopped
3oz (90g) sultanas
2½oz (75g) raisins, chopped
2 tablespoons rum

1. Place ice cream, apricots, cherries, pears, sultanas, raisins and rum in a bowl and mix to combine. Pour into a buttered and lined 6-cup capacity pudding basin.

2. Freeze for 3 hours or until firm.

NOTE
To help unmould the pudding, briefly hold a warm damp tea towel around the outside of the mould. To serve, slice pudding and serve with rum custard.

Truffle easter eggs

makes 32

9oz (250g) dark chocolate, melted
½ cup double cream
9oz (250g) milk chocolate
1 tablespoon golden syrup

1. Place a spoonful of dark chocolate in a small easter egg mould and use a small paint brush to evenly coat. Freeze for 2 minutes or until chocolate sets. Repeat with remaining chocolate to make 32 shells.

2. Place cream in a saucepan and bring to the boil. Remove pan from heat, add milk chocolate and stir until smooth. Stir in golden syrup and chill for 20 minutes or until mixture is thick enough to pipe.

3. Spoon filling into a piping bag (see page 17) fitted with a plain-shaped nozzle and pipe filling into chocolate shells. Cover filling with more melted chocolate and chill until set before removing from mould.

NOTE
Eggs can be moulded and filled several hours in advance. Store in a covered container in a cool, dry place.

Valentine's brownies

makes 12

1. Preheat oven to 350°F (180°C). Line a 7 x 11in (18 x 28cm) baking tin with foil and set aside.

2. Combine 1 cup flour and the sugar, then cut in butter until crumbly. Press onto bottom of pan. Bake for 15 minutes.

3. In another bowl, beat condensed milk, cocoa, egg, remaining ¼ cup flour, vanilla and baking powder. Mix in chocolate pieces and nuts. Spread over prepared crust and bake for 20 minutes or until set.

4. Cool and lift out of pan. Cut with heart-shaped cookie cutter or cut around a cardboard heart template using a knife. Decorate with icing if desired. Store in an airtight container.

1¼ cups all-purpose (plain) flour
¼ cup sugar
½ cup butter
14fl oz (400ml) condensed milk
¼ cup unsweetened cocoa powder
1 egg
1 teaspoon vanilla extract
½ teaspoon baking powder
9oz (250g) milk chocolate, broken into chunks
¾ cup chopped nuts

Christmas bombe alaska

serves 10

1. Remove ice cream from freezer and remove 2 cups from the centre, leaving a smooth cavity in the centre. Using a spoon dipped in hot water will help achieve a smooth shape.

2. Place the removed ice cream in a mixing bowl with chopped chocolate, hazelnut spread, nuts and fruit mince and mix well to combine. If ice cream has softened too much, freeze until firm enough to hold the fruit. Spoon fruit mixture into the cavity and press until smooth, then freeze again for at least 2 hours.

3. Remove from freezer and run a knife around the edge. If very frozen, dip the base into a sink of warm water.

4. Invert ice cream onto the sponge and cut around the sponge to meet the edge of the ice cream. Remove excess sponge and remove container from ice cream. Re-freeze until the meringue is ready.

5. Preheat oven to 465°F (240°C). Combine egg whites and cream of tartar and beat with electric mixer until soft peaks begin to form. Gradually begin adding the sugar, beating as you go, until a firm meringue is achieved.

6. Spread meringue all over frozen dessert and place in oven for 3–5 minutes or flash with a blow torch until meringue becomes crisp and golden. Serve at once.

70fl oz (2L) vanilla ice cream
3½oz (100g) dark chocolate, chopped
½ cup hazelnut spread
¼ cup toasted hazelnuts, chopped
¼ cup fruit mince
1 sponge cake
3 egg whites
1 teaspoon cream of tartar
¾ cup superfine (caster) sugar

Christmas stocking biscuits

makes 24

4oz (125g) butter
¾ cup powdered (icing) sugar
1 egg
1¼ cups all-purpose (plain) flour
1¼ cups self-rising (self-raising)
   flour
3oz (90g) dark chocolate, melted
2oz (60g) milk chocolate, melted
powdered (icing) sugar, for
   dusting

1. Preheat oven to 350°F (180°C). Place butter, icing sugar, egg, all-purpose flour and self-rising flour in a food processor and process until a soft dough forms. Knead dough briefly, wrap in cling wrap and chill for 30 minutes.

2. Roll out dough on non-stick baking paper to ⅛in (5mm) thick.

3. Using a template of a Christmas stocking or a Christmas stocking cookie cutter, cut stocking shapes and place on a buttered baking tray. Bake for 10 minutes or until biscuits are golden. Transfer to a wire rack to cool.

4. Dip tops of stockings in dark chocolate to make a ⅓in (1cm) border. Allow to set.

5. Dip biscuits into milk chocolate halfway up dark chocolate. Allow to set. Dust with powdered sugar.

NOTE

Use any leftover melted chocolate to pipe designs onto the stockings, if desired.

Easy chocolate tart

serves 8

1. Lightly grease the base of a 7¾in (20cm) springform tin.

2. Combine crushed biscuits and butter in a bowl. Press mixture into base of tin. Chill for 30 minutes until set.

3. Combine milk and dark chocolate in a microwave-safe bowl. Melt on medium (50%) power for 1 minute. Stir and return to oven for 30 seconds. Continue cooking in this way until melted and smooth. Mix in icing sugar. Set aside to cool slightly.

4. Fold cream through chocolate. Pour over biscuit base. Smooth top and chill for 5 hours or overnight, until set. Melt white chocolate, pipe or drizzle over tart and serve.

7oz (200g) plain sweet biscuits, crushed
3½oz (100g) butter, melted
150g milk chocolate, roughly chopped
5oz (150g) dark chocolate, roughly chopped
2 tablespoons powdered (icing) sugar, sifted
1¼ cups thickened cream, whipped
1¾oz (50g) white chocolate

Index

Published in 2013 by
New Holland Publishers
London • Sydney • Cape Town • Auckland

Garfield House 86–88 Edgware Road London W2 2EA United Kingdom
Wembley Square First Floor Solan Road Gardens Cape Town 8001 South Africa
1/66 Gibbes Street Chatswood NSW 2067 Australia
218 Lake Road Northcote Auckland New Zealand

www.newhollandpublishers.com

A catalogue record of this book is available at the British Library and the National Library of
Australia.

ISBN: 9781742573854

Publisher: Fiona Schultz
Design: Lorena Susak
Production Director: Olga Dementiev
Printer: Toppan Leefung Printing Ltd (China)

10 9 8 7 6 5 4 3 2 1

Texture: Shutterstock

Follow New Holland Publishers on
Facebook: www.facebook.com/NewHollandPublishers

UK £ 9.99
US $14.99